object
lessons

object
lessons

THE ROLE OF MUSEUMS IN EDUCATION

EDITED BY SUE MITCHELL

SCOTTISH
MUSEUMS
COUNCIL

EDINBURGH : HMSO

Application for reproduction should be made to HMSO

HMSO Scotland
21 South Gyle Crescent
Edinburgh
EH12 9EB

British Library Cataloguing in Publication Data
A catalogue record for this book is available from the British Library

The Scottish Museums Council is an independent company, principally funded by The Secretary of State for Scotland. The Council's mission is to improve the quality of museum and gallery provision in Scotland. This it seeks to do by providing a wide range of advice, services and financial assistance to its membership, and representing the interests of museums in Scotland.

Scottish Museums Council
County House
20-22 Torphichen Street
Edinburgh
EH3 8JB

tel. 0131-229 7465   fax. 0131-229 2728

0 11 495756 8

Contents

Contents

Foreword

Museums are the outcome of human curiosity, of the desire to learn. It is hard to imagine anyone visiting a museum for more than a few minutes without learning something new, whatever their age and whatever their formal educational background. Museums are resources for all kinds of learning and because their stock-in-trade is composed of objects, which can be seen and sometimes handled, they can have a greater immediacy of impact than most other learning resources if used imaginatively.

If you visit a museum purely for enjoyment, without any particular plan in mind, learning will be casual and random. If you visit with a plan (either yours or a teacher's or lecturer's) your learning becomes part of an educational activity. Museum education therefore is, in its broadest sense, organised learning activity which uses museum objects or collections to forward the learning process.

Museum education can involve full-time learners in schools, or part-time learners in further education, community education, the Open University, continuing professional development and others. It is about the promotion of lifelong learning. School-museum activities are critically important in this because if young people are taught to appreciate and use museums to satisfy their learning needs and stimulate their curiosity further, they will be aware of the value of museums for learning throughout their lives as well.

Educators and museum professionals are natural partners, who perhaps need to learn more of each other's methods. Educators may not be aware of the very wide capacities of museums to support learning across the curriculum and museum professionals may not always have thought through the best ways of stimulating planned learning through their displays. Together they can better fulfil the vision of ICOM, of museums as places of "study, education and enjoyment".

The Scottish Museums Council is committed to such a vision and the initiative described in this publication was planned, with member museums, to push it forward.

Lalage Bown
Chair, Scottish Museums Council

Introduction

The Museums Education Initiative is founded upon two convictions: the first is that education lies at the heart of the rationale for the existence of collections in the public domain; and the second is that the educational potential of many museums is largely untapped, most especially with respect to children during their formative years. The conviction that much more can be done was vividly illustrated by the first report of the Initiative, the *Survey of Current Practice in Museums Education in Scotland*, written by Katie Donnelly in June 1993. Of the museums surveyed, only 6% had full-time education officers seconded from the Regional Authority; 3% employed their own full-time education officer; and 16% had staff who had some measure of designated responsibility for education. Less than 13% of museums provided regular information to schools.

During the course of the Initiative it has become clear that there are exciting benefits for museums and schools once they identify their areas of mutual interest. This identification is predicated upon museum personnel understanding the needs of teachers and pupils, particularly in relation to the curriculum, and upon teachers gaining awareness of what museums can realistically offer and gaining confidence in the imaginative use of what for many are unfamiliar kinds of teaching material. On one hand, teachers and school managers need to be convinced that object-based study in museums offers such unique possibilities that time and money should be set aside. On the other hand, museum personnel need to be assured that behind the hideous jargon of current curriculum-speak there are real educational ideals with which they can work and to which they can productively devote their pressured time.

Confidence in museum education can only be founded on a recognition of the way in which items in collections and other kinds of museum displays can be encouraged to speak compellingly of origins, materials, uses, users, cultural values, the human and natural worlds and so on. Objects can speak to pupils in a different and more visually suggestive way than words, providing we learn how to use the visual. The process is an active, participatory one, and there is no part of the curriculum potentially untouched by museum collections.

Following the Survey, completed after the first of the Initiative's three years, Susan Mitchell has energetically pursued a series of pilot projects, designed to produce case studies of examples of good practice and to highlight the most and least productive experiences of the many participants. The projects embrace a wide range of types of museum and educational experience, bearing in mind geographical location, type and size of collection and exhibit, curriculum area, and educational materials. A major purpose is to ensure that each school and museum does not, in effect, have to invent the wheel anew, and that ideas can be drawn out of the studies to enable new local initiatives to proceed both creatively and economically.

The Initiative will only have met its full aims if continuing activity is stimulated. The Scottish Museums Council will be keen to see the point of publication as the end of the beginning rather than the beginning of the end of the Initiative. Anyone who has seen the apparently inert objects in a museum coming to life under the shining eyes of curious pupils, heard the buzz of discussion between children, teachers and curators, and witnessed the creative projects stimulated by a new kind of experience will know what is possible. The Initiative is intended, in all senses of the term, to produce object lessons for everyone in the museums and education communities.

Martin Kemp
Chair of the Advisory Panel on Education in Museums and Galleries

Editor's Note

The Museums Education Initiative (MEI) was founded on the conviction held by Timothy Ambrose, former Director of the Scottish Museums Council, that the changes taking place in the Scottish education system provided a fresh and exciting opportunity to promote the range of primary source material, housed within museums, as a significant resource for teachers. It was his vision that an Initiative be created which would encourage museums and galleries of all types to provide increased educational support for schools.

Object Lessons is the culmination of the MEI, intended as the means by which the experiences and lessons learned during the three-year programme are communicated to and can ultimately benefit a wider audience. It seeks to provide inspiration, practical help and advice for all museum and teaching staff wishing to realise the potential of museum collections to underpin the Scottish schools' curriculum.

Perhaps the main message to come out of the Initiative is that so much more can be achieved through collaboration with others. For that reason, *Object Lessons* begins with accounts of some of the partnership ventures through which interesting and exciting pilot projects developed as part of the MEI programme. Furthermore these pilot projects, which reflect the diversity of Scotland's museums, are used throughout the publication as exemplars. They illustrate the varied ways in which museum collections of all types can be used to meet the requirements of specific areas of the curriculum for pupils aged 5 to 18. A number of the pilot projects have been written up separately as detailed case studies and are available from the Scottish Museums Council.

Object Lessons is in itself a collaborative venture and I am grateful to all contributors, who are individually acknowledged within its pages. Moreover, the publication is a testament to the large number of people in museums and galleries, and other organisations throughout Scotland, who participated so enthusiastically in the Initiative. I am grateful for their commitment and for the immense personal support I received. Thanks must also go to Timothy Ambrose and Rosi Capper, former Assistant Director (Curatorial Services), for their much appreciated help and encouragement, and to Professor Martin Kemp and other members of the Council's Advisory Panel on Education in Museums and Galleries for their often much needed guidance.

It would not have been possible to establish and develop the Museums Education Initiative without considerable financial support, and the Scottish Museums Council is indebted to Highlands and Islands Enterprise, the MacRobert Trusts and the Dorothy Burns Charity who joined with them in funding the programme. Furthermore specific project funding was gratefully received from the Foundation for Sport and the Arts, Highlands and Islands Enterprise and BP in Scotland.

Sue Mitchell
Museums Education Initiative Co-ordinator

Photographs throughout the text are reproduced by permission of the Scottish Museums Council, participating museums, and BP in Scotland.

Part 1

PARTNERSHIP IS NOT AN OPTION
...it is an essential requirement for the future development of museum education

School groups have traditionally been, and continue to be, potentially one of the largest audiences for museums. A great strength of museum education has always been its ability to motivate and excite children, and to provide them with new learning experiences. However, the changing curriculum in Scottish schools has resulted in some changes in the pattern of visits to museums as teachers look for resources which directly support work being undertaken in the classroom. Corresponding changes have also been taking place in museums (to displays, the pattern of temporary exhibitions, loan collections and publications) in order to provide that support. These have generally been achieved through the joint efforts of educators and museum professionals.

The concept of educators and museum professionals working as partners, has been fundamental to the development of the Museums Education Initiative which was designed to stimulate museum education services in Scotland, with regard to formal education. The Survey of Current Practice in Museums Education in Scotland showed that 84% of the museums surveyed had minimal or no access to professional education staff and recommended that:

> "...communication between schools, museums and educational bodies be actively sought" Katie Donnelly (1993)

Through its series of pilot projects the Initiative has since fostered partnerships between museums, schools, local education authorities and other educational establishments, including those in industry. The following case studies illustrate the effectiveness of those partnerships in the development of museum education services for schools.

Case Study:

THE PARTNERSHIP APPROACH TO *OPERATION MOVE IT!* AT THE SCOTTISH MINING MUSEUM

Operation Move It! was the result of a careful evaluation process which measured the existing Scottish Mining Museum education provision against plans to meet and stimulate future demand. Central to this process was development in partnership with education advisors, teachers and specialists.

Communication between museum staff and educators was initiated by establishing an Education Working Party which first met in December 1993. Advice and opinion was sought for an educational programme to complement a planned exhibition called *The Challenges of Mining*, which would look at the science and technology of coal mining. Representatives were invited from local primary and secondary schools, the Scottish Consultative Council on the Curriculum (Scottish CCC), Lothian Regional Council Education Department, and the Scottish Office

Experimenting with pulleys.

Education Department. This gave a breadth of knowledge and a range of different perspectives on our proposals, which was essential as our brief was to create a new service which was relevant to the 5–14 curriculum.

Very valuable feedback was gathered from the Working Party which helped staff to familiarise themselves with current concepts and accommodate them in the development process. Without this our pack and activities on site would have missed out on exploiting some important opportunities. For example, the Working Party was able to redirect our quite proscriptive view of how the activity sessions should be used by groups. By introducing the concept of "differentiation", as gently explained by our experts, we re-wrote the pack, giving suggestions rather than instructions where appropriate to enable the sessions to be used in a flexible way for pupils of different levels of understanding and ability.

Operation Move It! looked to others in the education field to aid its development also, taking advantage of the Teacher Placement Service offered by Lothian Regional Council in conjunction with Understanding British Industry (UBI). This resulted in two teachers coming to the Museum on a week long placement in Spring 1994. We were fortunate in that one of the two teachers was employed at Newtongrange Primary School, in the village where the Museum itself is based. This was particularly useful, lending local understanding to the professional expertise. The teachers were briefed to evaluate the museum site and collections to identify suitable areas for activities linked to the chosen theme.

In general a very helpful and practical partnership is evolving between Newtongrange School and the Museum, encouraged by the Head Teacher who sits on the Museum Trust.

An advantage of this partnership is that it brings the Museum into contact with children as well as adults at the development stage. Pilot sessions helped us to assess our proposals by clearly indicating the children's capabilities, needs and interests. This was particularly useful when assessing the effectiveness of the hardware and how children reacted to it, for example whether it was suitable to their height and weight.

For the Museum these partnerships have turned out to be very positive experiences. The main overall benefit has been that they have enabled us to feel totally confident that the end product is right for the market, having been informed by current thinking and the needs of both pupils and teachers. We are now able to sell the service to our customers as such, rather than promoting an isolated development driven by a desire to increase visitor numbers.

Rosemary Everett
July 1995
Rosemary Everett is Keeper at the Scottish Mining Museum

Case Study:

TRACING THE DEVELOPMENT OF TWEEDDALE MUSEUM'S PARTNERSHIP WITH LOCAL SCHOOLS AND WITH BORDERS REGIONAL COUNCIL EDUCATION DEPARTMENT

Tweeddale Museum first began to include education in its remit in 1990. The creation of an education programme was influenced by the number and experience of the three part-time staff (a curator, exhibitions officer and museum assistant) and the size of Tweeddale District (a rural area, population 15,000, with 11 primary schools and one secondary school.)

Although the museum is run by a District Council which does not have responsibility for education, all the staff share a belief in museum education as:

●   a core function of the museum service;
●   a means of taking an active role in the community; and
●   a means fostering new and future audiences.

Initial contact with local schools was made via one-off visual arts projects, either as a way of interpreting the exhibition programme or of creating new work for exhibition. This helped establish a trust and understanding between schools but was dependent on one member of staff trailing round schools, meeting head teachers on a one-to-one basis, a time consuming and impractical way of working.

A new approach was instigated, in 1992, by a new member of staff, a replacement museum assistant who happened to be a qualified primary school teacher. Her knowledge of school procedures and education department structures introduced a clearer sense of direction. She began work on an education policy which would embrace the whole community, but which would focus initially on proactive provision for schools. The publication, *Writing an Education Policy,* by Eileen Hooper-Greenhill (Leicester University, 1991) provided basic guidelines which were further developed through discussions with local headteachers, the Regional Council's Primary Adviser and contacts in the Education Department of the National Museums of Scotland. The written policy was accepted by the District Council in 1992, and built into the museum's Development Plan 1993–96.

Practical help came from the Region's Primary Adviser in Drama.

The education policy recognised that:

> *"It is important to offer a service which can be integrated into the school curriculum."*

Practical tips came from the Primary Adviser:

- staff at the Teachers' Resource Centre hold lists of popular topics regularly studied in class;
- the programme of Channel 4 and BBC television and radio broadcasts for schools indicate likely topic choices for the year ahead;
- schools plan well in advance, therefore collaboration with local schools at the forward planning stage would be mutually beneficial; and
- Planned Activity Time (PAT), the weekly session laid aside by all schools for staff development, provides an ideal opportunity for interaction with teachers.

The museum began to provide handling boxes and/or sessions to tie in with class topics. When demand exceeded supply for a tremendously popular, oversubscribed fossil casting workshop created to support the topic of "Dinosaurs", an in-service training session equipped teachers to use the museum's fossil casting loan pack.

Aiming to be even more proactive, the museum researched into what was expected to be a popular topic in primary schools for 1993, one which the museum's collections would strongly support, and one which would interest other groups within the community. In August 1992, museum staff started to plan for a month-long 'hands-on' exhibition on the theme of mini-beasts, to take place in May 1993. The exhibition was to be open to the general public, with interpretive workshops for schools. A meeting with the Primary Adviser secured advice, staff participation, and funding from the Region.

Teachers were invited to a cheese and wine evening in September 1992 which presented the mini-beast project. Prototypes of 'hands-on' exhibits were demonstrated and discussed, with time for feedback and suggestions from teachers. The exhibition and workshops took place successfully, fully booked with a range of ages and schools from throughout the District taking part. Evaluation showed that the exhibition was also a big hit with all sections of the community, from pre-school groups to the elderly.

Similar projects took place over the next two years. Communication by letter and twice yearly meetings with the Adviser maintained support and funding. Support spread, with assistance in the planning and execution of projects coming from Primary Advisers in Environmental Studies, the Expressive Arts, and Maths. Post-project visits to schools by museum staff and analysis of questionnaire and interview results (with teachers and pupils) influenced the development of future projects. Continued face-to-face communication through teachers' evenings and school visits as well as through regular newsletters has maintained teacher interest and involvement. Links with Peebles High School are now being developed.

For Tweeddale Museum developing an education service has been a big commitment. Regional funding has never been guaranteed and the level of provision so far has possibly overstretched staff, but initial objectives have been met. A major factor in its success has undoubtedly been the partnerships developed with the Regional Council and at local level. It is hoped that changes in 1996, when the District will be subsumed within the present Region, will consolidate those partnerships and strengthen the position of education at Tweeddale Museum.

Rachel Hunter
July 1995
Rachel Hunter is Exhibitions Officer at Tweeddale Museum, Peebles

Case Study:

THE BENEFITS OF MUSEUM NETWORKING IN ROSS AND CROMARTY

It is hard to believe that it was only 16 months ago that the Co-ordinator of the Museums Education Initiative first visited Ross and Cromarty. So much has been achieved since then in making our museums more relevant to children and to school parties.

Ross and Cromarty is a large and essentially rural district, with tourism playing a major role in the economy of the area. The seven small local museums are run as independent charitable trusts and have to attract tourists as well as locals to achieve their target incomes.

We have a museums networking group, where representatives from each of these independent museums meet on an occasional basis for discussion, training and exchange of information. Even though our museums are all very different, they face similar challenges and opportunities within the local and the tourism framework. Rather than reinventing the wheel, we try to take a common approach where possible.

With the overall aim being to assist our museums in increasing the relevancy of their service to schools, the suggestion was that we do so initially by securing a teacher placement at three or four museums within the group, arranged through the Teacher Placement Service established by Understanding British Industry (UBI). The teacher looked at:

Understanding the Picts at Groam House, Rosemarkie.

- how the museums could make moves to better fit into the 5–14 curriculum;
- how the 5–14 curriculum best fits the museums of Ross and Cromarty;
- what local schools think of the current service offered by our museums; and
- what schools would like to see in the local museums.

David Charnley, the Education Liaison Officer for Understanding British Industry and Highland Regional Council's Education Department, was very helpful in setting up an evening to allow us to tempt teachers with the idea of taking on such a placement, and with providing the mechanism and the money whereby the whole thing was possible – such as cover for the teacher in the classroom during the period of the placement. We were taken by storm, however, by Catherine Mackay of Invergordon Park Primary, who came to the meeting already intending to be our placement and full of ideas, timescale, logistics and so on. She was a godsend to the project and is principally responsible for its success to date.

The Scottish Museums Council offered to match funding from Ross and Cromarty District Council (RCDC) up to £500 per museum from each of us, so the museums were looking at a possible £1,000 to spend on their final product and several days of Catherine's time to help them decide on what to go for.

All of our seven museums were invited to apply for the grant-aid, although for reasons of time and distance Catherine could only work with the cluster of four nearest to her home base. The advantage of the network group was that on training and update days, all were represented and information disseminated.

Sixteen months on, where are we? The original timetable was for June 1995 completion, which we have almost achieved. All of the projects should be ready for the schools and/or children visiting the museums by the start of the next session in August. It is worth stressing that none of the material is just for schools - other family visitors will benefit too. Projects include loans boxes, reproduction costume for role-play; hands-on activities incorporated into permanent displays; activity sheets; an open-ended play based on a local event; CD-ROM access to archives; demographic studies and teachers' resource packs. Three of our museums now also have comprehensive education policies.

The benefits are going to be felt by many parties:

- The museums get extra visitors, a more worthwhile experience for the younger visitors and extra clout when applying for grant-aid.
- Local – and not so local – schools get more of a sense of ownership of the museum, more relevant material accessed during visits, good pre- and post-visit materials and good local studies to fit into their curriculum.
- The resource material is fed into the Highland Region Curriculum Development Centre, for wider dispersal and expansion.
- Parents visiting the museums get a better deal, through their children being better occupied and informed.
- RCDC gets a cost effective way of delivering a part of its remit on outreach provision for the younger museum visitor and on museum development.
- Catherine gained enormously from the chance to get out of the classroom and to work on these projects alongside the museum curators, projects which she can now access back in the classroom situation.

Everyone involved in Ross and Cromarty's teacher placement project through the Museums Education Initiative has been impressed by what has been achieved in such a short space of time. Dave Charnley of Highland Region's Education Department has described our project as a model for teacher placements throughout the Highlands and has suggested that we should consider future placements to push the project even further. Our thanks must go to everyone concerned. Long may such collaborations continue.

Steve Callaghan
July 1995
Steve Callaghan is Assistant Heritage Officer with Ross and Cromarty District Council. His role is threefold: to advise the independent museums of Ross and Cromarty on policy, procedure and practice, to assist them with their outreach programmes and to run his own outreach programme throughout this large and essentially rural District.

Case Study:

UNITED WE STAND! – A 'HANDS ON' PARTNERSHIP IN MARISCHAL MUSEUM

Marischal Museum's Museum Education Initiative project was a research project which investigated the experiences of children during object handling workshops. It has been published as *Hands On! Children's learning from objects in Marischal Museum.* One of the important features of this project has been the range of partnerships which underpinned it – from before its inception to beyond its completion.

For many years school groups have visited the museum, sometimes to see the museum displays and increasingly to take part in workshops. During these workshops children are able to handle high quality authentic objects related to popular school projects. These include 'Victorians', 'Ancient Egyptians', 'Scottish Prehistory' and 'Senses'. As the museum does not have an education officer, partnerships underlay the development of these workshops. An example of this is seen in the 'Victorians' and 'Georgians' workshops. With advice and encouragement from the Aberdeen Urban Studies Centre (part of Grampian Region Education Department) handling collections were formed and information about the workshops produced for teachers taking part. It is now possible for teachers to arrange a whole day's activities making use of the services offered by both the Centre and Marischal Museum, and to make a single booking through the Centre. Building on this experience, handling collections were formed for the other workshops and a clear menu created with information leaflets written about the different workshops.

Neil Curtis aids pupil investigation of objects at Marischal Museum

Initially, workshops took place in the museum's exhibition galleries, but in 1993 a purpose-built activity area and auditorium was created. This was funded from a variety of sources including the University, charitable trusts and commercial sponsorship. One of the sponsors, Shell UK Exploration and Production, also offered to support the educational activities in the museum by redesigning and printing the workshop information leaflets in the form of an information folder. Thanks to Grampian Region Education Department offering the use of their internal mail system, these have now been distributed to all schools in the Region, and copies are given to all teachers who make an enquiry. This three-way partnership was also behind the production of a booklet, *Learning with Objects*, which has had a similar distribution. This was written by Kim Davidson, who was seconded from Slains Primary School for 40 days, and designed and printed by Shell Expro.

Evaluation forms are usually given to teachers at the end of a workshop to help the museum improve its educational service and to give information about the context in which visits take place. However, the views of the children taking part remained unexplored. The establishment of the Scottish Museums Council's Museum Education Initiative presented us with the opportunity to investigate the children's experiences through a formal research project. We also felt that such research could be of interest to other small museums with a similar approach to ourselves.

Without experience of educational research ourselves, we turned to Sydney Wood of Northern College, Aberdeen. Our links with the college had developed over a number of years as groups of students had used the museum to discover the value of museum education. The research proposal was developed in collaboration with Sydney Wood, and funding was sought from both the Scottish Museums Council and from Shell Expro. Both were keen to take part, with the result that 100% funding was available. The research was carried out by Janet Goolnik of Northern College and has resulted in a museum monograph which was launched along with *Learning with Objects*. The many people who had helped both projects were invited to the launch, while it was an opportunity to let other people know about the Museum's educational services. The results have also been published in other publications, such as the *Journal for Education in Museums*.

Although I have outlined the formal partnerships that have developed over the past few years, I have been struck by the network of support that now surrounds us. This has sometimes had concrete effects, as in the creation of a workshop related to Kathleen Fidler's book, *The Desperate Journey*, which followed discussion with a number of teachers, and the Schools Library Service contacting the museum for advice on the revision of their loans boxes. However, the greatest value of such partnerships is often unquantifiable. The museum has become more aware of who to turn to for advice and support, while the potential of the museum – and museum education in general – hopefully now occupies a more prominent place in the minds of many more people.

Neil G W Curtis
Neil Curtis is Assistant Curator at the Marischal Museum, University of Aberdeen

Case Study:

MUSEUMS IN PARTNERSHIP – FIFE MUSEUMS FORUM

In February 1982 the Council for Museums and Galleries in Scotland called a meeting in Fife to discuss setting up to the first Museum Consultative Committee in Scotland. Such committees had been advocated by the Museums and Galleries Commission in its 1978 report, *Framework for a System of Museums* (the Drew Report), as a means to *"work out plans to cover common interests and keep the provision of adequate museum facilities in the county under review"*. Fife was chosen not only for its diverse mix of local authority, university and independent museums, but also because a strong tradition of partnership had already developed, with shared publicity and informal exchange of curatorial advice and expertise.

The Fife meeting brought together representatives of the local authorities and museum organisations, all of whom welcomed the opportunity to formalise and further develop the existing pattern of mutual support. However, in a spirit of pioneering independence, they rejected the term 'Consultative Committee' in favour of 'Forum' as more accurately reflecting its purpose and so the Fife Museums Forum came into being.

The Forum's first concern was to define its policy and plan future developments. Following a survey of current museum resources and needs, the Forum decided to concentrate initially on a programme of coordinating collecting policies, conservation and design services and publicity. As far as museum education was concerned, the survey revealed that, although there were no established education posts, several museums did operate a loans service as well as providing worksheets, talks and guided tours to visiting schools. A suggestion put forward at the exploratory meeting that museums might combine to lobby the Regional Council for financial support for educational services was not followed up.

By 1988, however, Standard Grade arrangements and further proposed changes to the Scottish schools' curriculum and their implications for museums were causing some unease. Aware the Fife museums lacked the resources to support the level of service likely to be demanded, the Forum approached Fife Education Department for approval in principle for a post of a museums education officer who could liaise between local

A Second World War-time Kitchen at Kirkcaldy Museum.

schools and museums, help teachers make the best use of museum resources and develop study materials. The proposal was turned down on grounds of cost and, for the time being, put into abeyance.

In December 1989 the Forum reorganised itself into a two-tier structure, with a Curators' Group operating within and reporting to the full Forum. This move provided an opportunity for taking stock and resulted in the Forum drawing up a three-year development plan in which it committed itself to campaigning for a joint education service staffed by a liaison officer.

In October 1990 the Forum submitted a report to the Education Department. The report, *Museums Education in Fife: the case for a museum education officer*, set out the potential of museums as an educational resource and cited statistical evidence to demonstrate the use made of Fife museums by schools. At the same time it voiced fears that without specialist staff both educational and curatorial standards could suffer and drew attention to the recommendations made by the Museums & Galleries Commission in its 1986 report, *Museums in Scotland* (The Miles Report).

Despite the strong case presented, the Education Department once again felt unable to allocate funds to establish a new post. Instead, the Chief Educational Librarian, who had in fact been a very supportive member of the Forum since its inception, was given extra responsibility for developing links between museums and schools. Although this was not the outcome hoped for, the Forum felt that it could be regarded as an acknowledgement by the Education Department that such liaison arrangements were in fact necessary.

As a direct result of this arrangement, and at the instigation of the Liaison Officer, the Forum turned its attention to producing a joint information pack for teachers which was given funding by the Education Department. Entitled *Pots, Paintings and Parasols - a teacher's guide to Fife's museums and galleries*, the pack aimed to publicise the resources available in each museum in the Forum, while at the same time linking them to curriculum topics through a grid prepared by the Liaison Officer. In addition, it included detailed information about each museum, along with advice on arranging and getting the best out of class visits.

The research involved in preparing this pack encouraged museum staff to think about their collections, how they fitted in with the curriculum and how they could be used. It raised awareness not only of the individual museum's ability to resource the curriculum, but also of what resources other museums within Fife provided which could complement their own provision.

Finally completed in the spring of 1993, copies of the pack were distributed to every school in Fife. Market research has shown, however that it has not been effective in reaching the class teacher, and alternative methods of marketing the pack need to be sought.

As the written word had not been as successful as hoped in promoting the Forum's message to schools, the question now arose as to whether a visual demonstration of what museums had to offer might have more effect. The Scottish Museums Council's Museums Education Initiative provided a gratefully received opportunity to take this idea forward, one which the Education Department supported both with funding and with direct involvement of schools, pupils and staff. The content and proposed use of the Fife Museum Forum video, *A Class of Their Own: the museum as a learning resource*, is described elsewhere in this volume and need not be repeated here. All those who participated in planning and producing the video learned a great deal about good practice in the use of museum collections. At the time of writing, copies of the video are only just being distributed, so its effectiveness in bridging the gap between museums and schools remains as yet untested.

What of the future for the Forum? The way forward remains unclear, especially in the face of impending local government reorganisation, which, in the case of Fife, will result in four local authorities merging into one. Communiqués from the Education Department continue to rule out the appointment of a museum eduction officer for the foreseeable future. Meanwhile the Forum is about to consider a new development plan. Whether or not the campaign for a joint education service should be maintained and, if so, how it is to proceed, are matters still to be decided.

Marion Wood
July 1995
Marion Wood is Assistant Curator with North East Fife Museums Service

Case Study:
PEOPLE AT WORK IN GRANGEMOUTH

People at Work was inspired by the collections representing the traditional industries of the Falkirk area, which are held at Grangemouth Museum Workshop and Stores, a branch of the Museum Service of Falkirk District. The project involved working in partnership with BP at Grangemouth, developing resource materials and an exhibition at Grangemouth Museum Workshop which could be complemented by a visit to BP's Exhibition and Information Centre at Grangemouth, and the BP educational resource materials used in the classroom.

People at Work invites pupils aged 10 to 14 to consider the development of agriculture, crafts and trades, and heavy industry around Falkirk and Grangemouth. BP's presence in Grangemouth is put into historical perspective as part of the working life of the Forth Valley. Pupils are thus helped to develop informed attitudes to the local environment.

People at Work is an excellent facility and resource to the public, teachers, pupils and education as a whole. The success of the project is due to a combination of factors but primarily there was something in the project for each of the partners: the Scottish Museums Council gained access to funding from BP for a project which furthered the aims of the Museums Education Initiative; Falkirk District Council Museums Service increased public access to an underused, yet extremely important collection; Central Region Education Department gained access to an excellent resource which supports Environmental Studies 5–14; and BP at Grangemouth benefited from good publicity, and better use of their facilities.

BP was approached and subsequently attracted to the project, firstly, because the company has been operating in Grangemouth since 1924 and secondly, because they viewed it as a worthy venture. BP is the largest employer in the area and having a *People at Work* exhibition in Grangemouth without BP would have been unthinkable, a great loss to the community and a lost opportunity for BP.

The main items that influenced BP to come on board were as follows:

- basic concepts were clarified from the outset;
- financial implications were clearly defined from day one;
- the project would involve BP facilities;
- it was a true genuine partnership approach.

Launch of *People at Work* at Grangemouth Museum Workshop and Stores.

From the outset, BP were extremely impressed by the professional approach adopted by our partners Scottish Museums Council and Falkirk District Museums. Meetings were kept to an absolute minimum and target dates were clearly identified and maintained. Agreed actions were implemented on time without fuss. All decisions were taken collectively and it was truly a partnership in progress.

The launch of the project itself took place on BP Company premises and a representative from each of the partners addressed the opening ceremony. Following the official launch a shuttle bus service took VIPs and guests to see the project. During the morning, pupils from local Grangemouth schools visited the project and participated in the photocall as well as having a look around the exhibition.

A week after the launch, the Museums Education Officer organised an in-service day for teachers and schools. Once again the partnership approach was in operation as BP was given an invitation to participate in the in-service training.

One of the problems facing schools at the moment is the high cost of hiring transport. The layout of *People at Work* requires small numbers to be effective. Given that BP has its main exhibition centre a few hundred yards from the Museum Workshop, it could be possible to co-ordinate a visit using the combined resources available and swapping pupils over. That way larger groups of pupils could take advantage of the project and, in turn, transport costs become viable.

Building on the experience gained over this project the following points could be considered by those proposing to approach business for help and support:

- Ensure your 'Aims and Objectives' for the project are clearly defined and realistic with built-in time scales.
- Requests for funding should be detailed and accurate. Allow plenty of notice; many companies plan their grants and donations well in advance.
- The 'Partnership' approach will probably be the preferred route for companies. A number of companies are moving away from the cheque book culture to the partnership approach. Make sure there is something in the project to attract the company.
- Remember that the person you are dealing with may have to sell or convince his/her boss that the project is worthy of support, so ensure that all the facts and costs are up front from the start and there are no major deviations in terms of initial costs.

The partners to the Grangemouth project have been extremely fortunate to put together this very worthwhile project for the benefit of the population of the Forth Valley. It has been a privilege and pleasure to work with such a talented team.

Francis B McKeever
July 1995
Francis McKeever is Co-ordinator of Education Links at BP at Grangemouth

THE PARTNERSHIP APPROACH

WITH WHOM?	WHAT FOR?
Local education authorities	• Advice about curricular links to local collections • Access to in-service training for teachers • Advice and practical support for individual projects • Possible funding for projects
Local schools	• To ensure relevancy of provision to local needs • Familiarisation visits to schools for museum staff • Advice during product development • Piloting of activities and resource materials by pupils • Access to teachers during Planned Activity Time
Other educational organisations, such as: Colleges of Education; Universities; UBI; Scottish CCC.	• Research projects into museum education • Access to pre-service teacher training • Update on developments in Scottish education • Providing opportunities for staff/curriculum development which encourage mutual understanding
Other museums	• Pooling resources, skills and knowledge • Dissemination of ideas and experiences • Building up a network of contacts
Industry	• Raising funds for projects • Extending the resources available to the museum through sponsorship in kind • Obtaining mutually beneficial publicity

Part 2

MUSEUMS AND SCHOOLS
...collections and the curriculum

AN OVERVIEW OF THE SCOTTISH SCHOOLS' CURRICULUM

The delivery of the school curriculum in Scotland is the responsibility of the education authorities and individual schools. In practice, the existence of much national guidance on the content of the curriculum and of a single examining body has led to a broad consensus of what should be taught. Central guidance to education authorities is issued in the form of circulars from the Scottish Office Education Department (SOED), reports by HM Inspectors of Schools (HMIs) and advice from the Scottish Consultative Council on the Curriculum (Scottish CCC). Members of the Scottish CCC are appointed by the Secretary of State from a variety of backgrounds, and are charged with reviewing, developing and providing guidance on curricular matters to the Secretary of State and thereafter to schools. Each school works out programmes and selects courses that are suited to the needs of its own pupils and the local community.

The curriculum is not just about learning facts and developing skills. Children have to learn how to co-operate with and understand other children, how to acquire healthy habits and attitudes, how to understand rules, rights and responsibilities, how to value enterprise and competition, how to solve problems and make decisions, and how to care for the environment. These things are learned not only in the classroom; parents, the local community and the media all contribute to these wider aspects of the curriculum.

In recent years the curriculum in Scotland has been undergoing enormous change. Currently, there are three major government initiatives which have a bearing on the curriculum of schools. These are:

- the 5–14 Programme, which as its title indicates, is concerned with pupils in primary and in the early years of secondary schooling;
- the 'Higher Still' Development Programme, which is concerned with the reform of upper secondary school [S5–S6]; and, more indirectly,
- the introduction of devolved school management, the system whereby individual schools are delegated 80% of their local education authority budget, giving teachers, school boards, and parents opportunities to take decisions at a local level and to determine their spending priorities.

The curriculum for the years S3 and S4 in secondary are described in the Standard Grade arrangements which have been in place for some years.

Similar reforms have been on-going in England, Wales and Northern Ireland where museums have played a significant role in helping schools to implement the more rigid National Curriculum for 5-to-16-year-olds. The recent review of the National Curriculum has increased opportunities, particularly in primary schools, for teachers to develop their own programmes of work outside the National Curriculum. This grants teachers of the National Curriculum an element of the flexibility currently enjoyed by those in Scotland implementing the 5–14 National Guidelines which provide opportunities for teachers to exercise professional judgement within a flexible framework. Any such reforms which alter the way in which schools are run also have an effect upon those organisations, such as museums, which seek to provide support. Thus museums in England, Wales and Northern Ireland will also need to show similar flexibility to Scottish museums in responding to local needs.

The schools' curriculum in Scotland, as throughout the United Kingdom, is encouraging: investigative learning; exploration of the world beyond the classroom; and the use of primary sources. Museums are in a unique position to provide these experiences. Museum professionals and educators stand at a watershed, with the chance to reshape the involvement of museums with education. Together they need to take a closer look at the curriculum at all stages, from primary through to the end of secondary school, to identify the ways in which they can harness the sense of wonder and delight experienced by children when they are exposed to museum collections and use it to attain progression in learning.

Ronnie Armstrong
July 1995
Ronnie Armstrong is Assistant Director at the Scottish Consultative Council on the Curriculum

The 5–14 Curriculum

Traditionally the majority of school groups visiting museums have come from primary education. Any changes in the curriculum for this age group will clearly have implications for museums.

The aim of the 5–14 programme in general has been to provide clear guidance on **"what"** and **"how"** pupils should be learning in primary schools, and in the first two years of secondary education. It is founded on the good practice already evident in Scottish schools, and seeks to provide a broad, balanced, and coherent approach to learning which ensures continuity during the first nine years of schooling, developing the skills and knowledge of children between the ages of 5 and 14 through a progressive framework of ability levels.

"WHAT" PUPILS SHOULD BE LEARNING

The 5–14 curriculum is about the entitlement of all pupils: to acquire knowledge and understanding in a variety of subject areas; to develop appropriate skills and attitudes; and to develop personal and social skills. It provides a framework to encourage a structured and integrated approach to all these facets of learning and ensures sufficient **breadth** (wide range of areas of learning) by including all the main subject areas, and organising them into five curricular areas: Language; Mathematics; Environmental Studies; Expressive Arts; and Religious and Moral Education. The whole curriculum should contribute to the personal and social development of the child.

These curricular areas remain as such in the primary school, but translate into eight naturally linked modes in the secondary school which further articulate with the provision for Standard Grade courses in S3 and S4. As a means towards ensuring **balance** (enough time for each area of learning), an indication is given as to the proportion of time in schools which should be devoted to each curricular area or mode.

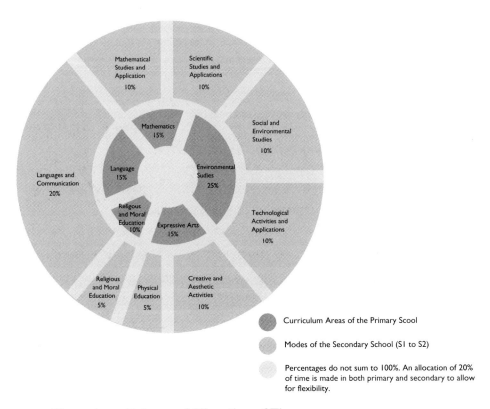

Curriculum Areas of the Primary Scool

Modes of the Secondary School (S1 to S2)

Percentages do not sum to 100%. An allocation of 20% of time is made in both primary and secondary to allow for flexibility.

Figure 1   Balance of Allocation of Time

National Guidelines give advice on each area of the curriculum. The guidelines set out **attainment outcomes** (broad competences within each curricular area), which relate to the component parts. These are further divided into a number of **strands** (aspects of learning which pupils will experience). Many areas and aspects of the 5–14 curriculum are inter-related and the guidelines give advice on programmes of study which will enable teachers, through careful planning, to make the connections, thus ensuring **continuity and coherence** (that the bits of learning fit together). See page 19.

Attainment targets (specific goals for learning within the individual strands), are based on five levels, A rising to E, which are intended to ensure **progression** (challenging but attainable goals which keep taking learning forward). Further guidance for progression in learning beyond level E is also provided.

In addition, National Guidelines give clear advice on personal and social development, assessment of learning, and reporting to parents and others.

"HOW" PUPILS SHOULD BE LEARNING

Teaching is about providing structured opportunities for pupils to learn. The 5–14 curriculum guidelines indicate the kinds of experiences which promote effective learning. The importance of providing a context for learning is emphasised, as is experiential learning which encourages pupils to plan, carry out and report on tasks which may involve them in observing at first hand or taking part in fieldwork. Teachers are encouraged to help pupils develop investigative skills by searching for evidence, speculating, and testing hypotheses. They are further encouraged to provide activities which will help pupils to develop their powers of creativity, imagination and expression.

These and other approaches to learning and teaching all have their place, and teachers are encouraged to be flexible, selecting for each group of pupils the method or methods best suited to achieving the learning objectives which have been identified.

WHAT ARE THE IMPLICATIONS FOR THE USE OF MUSEUMS AND THEIR COLLECTIONS?

"The levels of knowledge, understanding and skills development recommended in these guidelines will require teachers and pupils to draw upon a substantial and wide-ranging variety of evidence from beyond the classroom."

NATIONAL GUIDELINES,
ENVIRONMENTAL STUDIES 5–14

"The world beyond the school offers a wealth of resources for pupils and teachers...for example to art galleries, theatres, museums...pupils benefit enormously from being taken out into their local communities and environment."

NATIONAL GUIDELINES,
EXPRESSIVE ARTS 5–14

The National Guidelines recognise the value, and are actively promoting the use of resources outwith school. Teachers and museum staff already involved in museum education will read **"how"** pupils should learn with interest and immediately make the connection between the recommendations of the 5–14 curriculum and what museums have to offer by way of motivating pupils through their collections and providing opportunities of the types described for effective learning.

However, the clarification of primary school and early secondary school education through the introduction of the 5–14 curriculum, and the expectation that teachers should help pupils to achieve progression in learning, means that museum staff also need to address **"what"** pupils should learn. The implementation of the 5–14 Curriculum Guidelines has resulted in the necessity for a museum visit and use of the collections as a resource to be fully integrated into classroom studies.

In primary schools in particular, teachers often adopt a cross-curricular strategy, linking areas of the curriculum around a central theme or topic, thus providing a meaningful context for learning. A carefully planned museum visit can consolidate this type of study, with collections enriching that context through support for one or more areas of the curriculum. If museum staff are aware of what is to be studied in class they will be able to match their collections to particular topics and tailor their service to local needs. Equally so, if teachers are aware of what the museum has to offer as a resource it may influence their choice of topic.

The continuous and progressive nature of the 5–14 curriculum seeks to ensure that courses in secondary schools should carry on from the P7 experience, and so prevent the hiatus in learning which has often been observed at this stage. Secondary schools, therefore will need to consider the cross-curricular and cross-sectoral implications. Greater inter-departmental co-operation may lead to greater flexibility in timetabling, and one of the main stumbling blocks in attracting secondary school groups to museums may be removed.

ATTAINMENT OUTCOMES

ENGLISH LANGUAGE	MATHEMATICS	RELIGIOUS AND MORAL EDUCATION	PERSONAL AND SOCIAL DEVELOPMENT	ENVIRONMENTAL STUDIES DEVELOPMENT	EXPRESSIVE ARTS
Listening	Problems-Solving & enquiry	Christianity	Personal Development	*Science* Understanding living things and the processes of life	*Art & Design* Using materials techniques, skills and media
Talking		Other World Religions			
Reading	Information Handling		Social Development		Expressing feelings ideas, thoughts and solutions
Writing	Number, money measurement	Personal Search in Relation to:		Understanding energy and forces	
					Evaluating & appreciating
	Shape, position & movement			Understanding earth and space	
					Drama Using materials techniques, skills and media
				Social Subjects Understanding people and place	
					Expressing feelings, ideas, thoughts and solutions
				Understanding people in the past	
					Evaluating & appreciating
				Understanding people in society	
					Music Using materials techniques, skills and media
				Technology Understanding and using technology in society	
					Expressing feelings, ideas, thoughts and solutions
				Understanding and using the design process	
					Evaluating & appreciating
				Health Education Healthy and Safe Living	
					Physical Education Using materials techniques, skills and media
				Information	
				Technology Understanding and Using Information Technology	Expressing feelings, ideas, thoughts and solutions
					Evaluating & appreciating

ATTAINMENT OUTCOMES

Language 5–14

National Guidelines relating to the curricular area of Language in the 5–14 programme, are produced for English, modern European foreign languages, Gaelic and Latin.

Any classroom study which links areas of the curriculum around a central theme will be underpinned by language:

"Language is at the heart of children's learning. Through language they receive knowledge and acquire skills. Language enables children both to communicate with others effectively for a variety of purposes and to examine their own and others' experiences, feelings and ideas, giving them order and meaning. Because language is central to children's intellectual, emotional and social development, it has an essential role across the curriculum and helps pupils' learning to be coherent and progressive. Children's earliest language is acquired in the home and schools will build on that foundation."

NATIONAL GUIDELINES, ENGLISH
LANGUAGE 5–14 AND GAELIC 5–14

The 5–14 curriculum recognises that in many communities English is not the language spoken at home and encourages the development of bilingualism in today's multicultural society. In the Highlands and Islands of Scotland the use of Gaelic is widespread with classes conducted in the Gaelic medium on the increase. National Guidelines for both English Language 5–14 and Gaelic Medium 5–14 give guidance on four **attainment outcomes**: Listening; Talking; Reading and Writing. The **strands** within these outcomes are described identically in the guidelines outlining the kinds of activities which will lead to progression in learning from level A to level E. Teachers are furthermore encouraged to provide learning activities, balancing these outcomes, within a context – a real or imaginary situation which motivates pupils and provides a framework for learning.

Case Study:

A *Time to Keep* in the Western Isles

Museum nan Eilean, in the Western Isles, is fully bilingual and places great emphasis on working with the network of Comann Eachdraidh (Local Historical Societies), many of which operate village museums.

The project, A *Time to Keep*, illustrated the potential of museum collections to provide a context for a cross-curricular classroom study. It specifically considered how museums can extend pupils' vocabulary and grant opportunities to make use of spoken and written language. The project was conducted in Gaelic, but the activities were entirely appropriate for a similar study in English or any other language. Furthermore it raised awareness of the meaning of heritage. Thus the project can be used as a model for other areas of the United Kingdom where English may not be the language spoken in the home.

The idea for an educational initiative for schools, which could provide an adaptable model for museums and schools across Scotland, arose during the training course, 'Museum Basics: An Introduction to Preventive Conservation', held in Stornoway by the Scottish Museums Council. This was attended not only by the Education Officer and the other two staff members of the museum service, but also by volunteers within the Comann Eachdraidh.

A project was conceived which would:

Using gloves to handle objects at Nis.

- be undertaken in the Gaelic medium;
- focus on the preventive conservation of objects as a context for learning across the curriculum;
- introduce pupils to the meaning of heritage; and
- alert pupils to the role played by the museums and historical societies in preserving the Gaelic heritage of the Western Isles.

The project targeted pupils aged 10 to 14 years, involving one secondary and its associated primary schools with Comann Eachdraidh Nis (Ness Historical Society) on Lewis.

The whole project focused on the preventive conservation of objects. It started with pupils bringing into school, and talking about, objects which were precious to them and their families and which they would like to keep for future generations. Through a series of scientific experiments they identified potential threats to the conservation of those objects and how they might minimise the risk of damage. A visit to Comann Eachdraidh Nis encouraged pupils to use the knowledge and understanding they had gained to consider the role of museums in helping to preserve the heritage of local communities for future generations. Furthermore they were able to identify the problems the museums faced in looking after two and three dimensional objects, and make an assessment of the conditions in which artefacts at Nis were displayed and stored. As a follow-up activity Comann Eachdraidh Nis laid aside an area for the schools to exhibit their own objects and project work.

As the project was undertaken in the Gaelic medium, it was important to attain progression within the **attainment outcomes** of Listening, Talking, Reading and Writing as described in the National Guidelines Gaelic 5–14, Part 1 – Gaelic Medium Education and Gaelic for Fluent Speakers:

OUTCOME	STRANDS	PRESENT OWN OBJECTS IN CLASS	IDENTIFY DAMAGE THREATS ETC.	MUSEUM VISIT	EXHIBIT OWN OBJECTS & WORK
Listening	for information, instructions & directions		●	●	●
	in groups	●	●	●	●
	in order to respond to texts		●		
	awareness of genre				
	knowledge about language	●	●	●	●
Talking	conveying information, instructions & directions		●	●	●
	in groups	●	●	●	●
	about experiences, feelings, opinions	●		●	●
	about texts				●
	audience awareness	●		●	●
	knowledge about language	●	●	●	●
Reading	for information		●	●	●
	for enjoyment				●
	to reflect on the writer's ideas/craft				
	awareness of genre				
	reading aloud		●	●	
	knowledge about language		●	●	●
Writing	functional writing		●	●	●
	personal writing	●			●
	imaginative writing				●
	punctuation and structure	●	●		●
	spelling	●	●		●
	handwriting and presentation	●	●		●
	knowledge about language	●	●	●	●

The project worked well as a cross-curricular study. There were direct links to the Science and Social Subjects components of Environmental Studies. Information gathered about the objects had to be collected, organised, displayed, and interpreted, thus addressing the Information Handling **attainment outcome** of Mathematics. Using environmental monitoring equipment involved pupils in making mathematical calculations as well as illustrating applications of Technology. Pupils designed an exhibition of their own work, linking into Expressive Arts, Art and Design. Considering other ways of preserving Gaelic culture provided opportunities to link into Music and Drama and further into Language through literature. Looking at the wider interpretation of the word 'conservation' led pupils to develop informed attitudes about issues raised in contemporary life, such as the effects of pollution, the role of organisations such as Greenpeace, and the 'Save the Whale' campaign. In this way the project linked directly to Environmental Education which is concerned with the interaction between people and the environment, promoting concern for the needs of the environment, and action to conserve and improve it. The idea of human responsibility for past and future generations was thus developed, targeting the Personal Search **attainment outcome** in Religious and Moral Education.

An information/resource pack for schools on preventive conservation was prepared in Gaelic. This included: factsheets for teachers; pupil activity sheets; alignment to the 5–14 curriculum; suggestions for language activities and scientific experiments to do in the classroom; and suggestions for the integration of a museum visit. This resource pack has since been produced bilingually to allow for adaptation by museums throughout Scotland.

WHAT DID THIS PROJECT DO

...for the teachers:

- It provided a rich context for learning for language and other curricular areas.
- It raised their awareness of museums as a resource.
- It provided support materials for the development of Gaelic.

...for the pupils:

- It helped them to develop confidence and pleasure in their own use of Gaelic.
- It enabled them to attain progression in Listening, Talking, Reading and Writing in Gaelic and in other areas of the curriculum.
- It raised their awareness of the meaning of heritage and the part museums have to play in the preservation of that heritage.
- It gave them the scientific knowledge and skills to be able to set up their own exhibitions, taking into account the conservation needs of objects.
- It enabled them to develop both personally and socially.

...for staff in museums and historical societies:

- It helped to establish links locally between schools and the historical society.
- It reinforced previous training in preventive conservation.
- It raised awareness of the work of the historical society within the local community.

...for museums and schools throughout the United Kingdom:

- It has provided a model which, with its materials now produced bilingually, can be adapted for use across the United Kingdom.

Checking environmental monitoring equipment at Nis.

Environmental Studies 5–14

The area of the curriculum most likely to attract teachers to use museums as a resource is Environmental Studies, in that the National Guidelines for that curricular area strongly advocate fieldwork outwith the classroom. Fieldwork being used in a broad sense to include use of museums.

"The provision of first-hand experience through fieldwork for pupils is central to the methodology of Environmental Studies."

NATIONAL GUIDELINES,
ENVIRONMENTAL STUDIES 5–14

Environmental Studies groups together those aspects of study which are particularly founded on the pupil's observation of his or her surroundings. Through this curricular area, pupils both learn about the world around them and develop the knowledge, understanding, skills and attitudes necessary to interpret it.

Children do not experience their environment in separate subject terms. The social and physical environment interact with each other. However, for organisational purposes Environmental Studies is divided up into five components or subject areas. In each component suggested learning is divided into a number of **attainment outcomes** as are all areas of the 5–14 curriculum.

COMPONENT	ATTAINMENT OUTCOME
Science	Understanding living things and the processes of life Understanding energy and forces Understanding Earth and Space
Social Subjects	Understanding people and place Understanding people in the past Understanding people in society
Technology	Understanding and using technology in society Understanding and using the design process
Health Education	Healthy and safe living
Information Technology	Understanding and using information technology

Environmental Studies 5–14 differs from other curriculum guidelines in that each **attainment outcome** has an additional number of **key features** which provide guidance on the knowledge or skills which should be learned, or the contexts which should be used. Descriptions of the **key features**, and the contexts and content for developing understanding, can be found in the Environmental Studies 5–14 National Guidelines. These descriptors can be a useful tool for museum staff. Initially they may look daunting, but it is worth taking the time to work through them as they can stimulate ideas as well as ensure greater relevancy of the museum visit to what is actually happening in the classroom.

Within the **attainment outcomes** a framework of **strands** is used to help identify key aspects of learning which will be developed through participation in a wide range of learning activities. Of particular relevance to working with museum collections are the **strands** in Science, Social Subjects and Technology which include:

- Knowledge and understanding
- Planning
- Collecting evidence
- Recording and presenting (Science and Social Subjects only)
- Applying skills and presenting solutions (Technology only)
- Interpreting and evaluating
- Developing informed attitudes.

Environmental Education, which is concerned with the interaction between people and the environment, should be distinguished from Environmental Studies which gives pupils the knowledge and skills to be able to interpret the environment. Environmental Education is closely associated with the **strand** 'Developing informed attitudes'. Through attention to this **strand** pupils are encouraged to develop responsible attitudes to the environment as they gain wider knowledge, experience and understanding of it, and to recognise the importance of a system of sustainable development: that is, development which meets today's needs without adversely affecting future generations.

Examples drawn from projects undertaken by three museum services in different parts of Scotland illustrate the use of very different types of collections to support components of Environmental Studies.

Case Study:
1891 AT DINGWALL MUSEUM

The 'Victorians' is a popular cross-curricular study undertaken by teachers in primary schools, and one which museums are often asked to resource. The collections and displays of the small independent local museum at Dingwall include a Victorian kitchen and smiddy, and strongly support the theme of 'Victorians'. This seemed an appropriate place to begin to develop an education service for schools.

Taking the census of 1891 as their starting point, the curator and a local teacher on placement identified four families of differing social class who had lived in the town in the late 19th century and whose homes still exist today. They built up a profile of each family from evidence in the museum's collection: documents; household objects; personal artefacts; original photographs of

A Victorian 'family' at home in Dingwall Museum.

the houses and some of the people; and the tools and equipment in the smiddy which belonged to one of the families identified. A display on a local celebrity, Sir Hector Macdonald, who had lived at that time, was drawn into the project. Moreover, a newly-created Victorian town trail embraces the monument built in his memory and the home of each family. A resource pack for teachers includes extracts from the original sources including census records, local newspapers, photographs, school log books and OS maps. The prime use of the pack is for upper primary school pupils to assist with pre-visit and follow-up work in the classroom. During a visit the pupils 'become' members of one of the four families, dressing up in reproduction clothes, and collect evidence about their family in the museum and on the town trail.

The museum has chosen to specifically target the **attainment outcome**, Understanding People in the Past within the Social Subjects component of Environmental Studies, leaving teachers to make further curricular links appropriate to their own study.

ATTAINMENT OUTCOME	KEY FEATURES
Understanding People in the Past	• studying people, events and societies of significance in the past • developing an understanding of change and continuity over time • developing an understanding of time and historical sequence • developing an understanding of the nature of historical evidence • considering the meaning of heritage and the influence of the past upon the present

With regard to the framework of **strands**, the project at Dingwall Museum provides opportunities for pupils to plan what they want to investigate. During the visit they are involved in **collecting evidence**. They can **record and present** the results of their findings in a variety of ways, through drawing and painting, making models, taking photographs, through taking notes for more detailed written work back in the classroom, through drama and in oral descriptions. **Interpreting and evaluating** the information they collect enables pupils to build up a picture of how the Victorians lived, and during the course of the visit they are enabled to **develop informed attitudes** to the environment.

Experimenting with the technology of weaving in prehistory.

Case Study:

In Touch With the Past at Tweeddale Museum

The project, *In Touch With the Past*, was inspired by the exhibition of the same name on loan to Tweeddale Museum, Peebles, from Glasgow Museums. This exhibition of prehistoric tools was originally conceived for the visually impaired and its emphasis on touching and handling objects provided an ideal starting point for a museum education project involving archaeology. Tweeddale Museum used its own prehistory collections to complement and extend the exhibition, creating five separate interactive workstations which encouraged the investigation of Early People and their environment. Activities of varying complexity were designed to offer flexibility in dealing with pupils from P1 to P7, and for pupils with special needs.

A classroom study of Early People clearly provides opportunities to link into all areas of the 5–14 curriculum. However, *In Touch With the Past* placed a strong emphasis on science and technology, looking at the development of tools, the materials they were made from, and their uses in the home, in hunting, and in building shelter. Moreover, pupils were encouraged to speculate about the lives of Early People, using the archaeological remains as evidence. Thus the project concentrated on providing experiences which would support the Science, Social Subjects and Technology components of Environmental Studies. An alignment to each of these components was included in the preparatory information pack available for teachers. Two supporting packs were produced. The first being for teachers of P1–3 classes, the second for teachers of P4–7.

An example of the **key features** selected from the Technology component which the interactive workstations underpinned, is as follows:

ATTAINMENT OUTCOME	KEY FEATURES
Understanding and using technology in society	• Technology and human needs • Technology and demand for resources • Technology as it affects lifestyles • Technology to control the environment
Understanding and using the design process	• Properties of materials and tools in relation to their practical use • Devices and tools associated with control and their applications

Case Study:

OPERATION MOVE IT! AT THE SCOTTISH MINING MUSEUM

Operation Move It! is all about science and technology and how it has been used in the Scottish coal mining industry to move men, coal and materials up and down and around a mine.

Plans for a new exhibition at the Scottish Mining Museum which would look at the applied science and technology of the coal industry, stimulated ideas for an educational initiative for schools focusing on the Science and Technology components of Environmental Studies.

Operation Move It! presents children with five practical 'hands-on' problem solving activities, using large working models of mining machinery, which encourage curiosity about how technology meets needs, and explores the basic scientific principles of gears, pulleys, slopes, gravity and friction. Each experiment is clearly set out in its coal mining context and the models replicate machinery seen by pupils on a tour of the colliery.

The experiments are planned to link directly to the Science component of Environmental Studies with reference to P4–S2. In particular they relate very closely to an individual key feature and its detailed description in the guidelines.

ATTAINMENT OUTCOME	KEY FEATURE	CONTEXTS & CONTENT FOR DEVELOPING UNDERSTANDING P4-S2
Energy and forces	Forces and their effects	• friction forces on different surfaces • reducing friction • force of gravity • motion down a slope under gravity • simple pulley systems • simple gear systems • measurement of forces, spring balance • unit of force – the Newton (N)

In addition, pupils are encouraged to record their observations, estimates and results and thereby assist their understanding of technology and the demand for resources.

What difference do gears really make?

Mathematics 5–14

Museums have been shown to provide teachers with a real-life context for developing knowledge and understanding, and skills required for learning, in Environmental Studies. The National Guidelines also promote the use of contexts for learning mathematics:

"Children's motivation in mathematical activities and perceptions of the subject will be affected by the choice of contexts for learning."

NATIONAL GUIDELINES,
MATHEMATICS 5–14

Mathematics provides much more than the ability to calculate. It enables information to be handled and communicated, and problems to be solved, thus helping children to understand better the world about them. Furthermore Mathematics 5–14 encourages the use of a variety of contexts for learning in different aspects of mathematics which enable pupils to:

- develop skills in approaches to problem solving and enquiry,
- learn concepts, facts and techniques, needed to use and apply Mathematics in areas such as information handling; number, money and measurement; shape, position and movement,
- understand how the concepts, facts and techniques relate to one another.

In Mathematics, suggested learning is divided into four **attainment outcomes**:

- Problem-solving and enquiry
- Information handling
- Number, money and measurement
- Shape, position and movement.

The first of these, **problem-solving and enquiry,** develops the skills needed to approach mathematical situations which involve speculating about what to do. Each of the other **attainment outcomes** covers a different aspect of knowledge, ie concepts, facts and techniques, which it is necessary to learn to be able to solve the problem.

By providing a pleasurable context for learning in mathematics, museums can help to promote confidence and enjoyment in the subject.

Case Study:

LIFE AND DEATH IN MEDIEVAL PEEBLES, TWEEDDALE MUSEUM

After the success of *In Touch With the Past*, staff at Tweeddale Museum felt they would like to extend their own knowledge of the 5–14 curriculum, and at the same time show teachers that museums could provide a context for learning in areas of the curriculum other than environmental studies.

The next planned project for schools in Tweeddale focused on what life would have been like in Peebles in the Middle Ages, and it was realised that an emphasis on Mathematics was entirely appropriate in association with life in a medieval burgh. For the duration of the project the Picture Gallery was transformed into a medieval burgh with key buildings set around a market-place. With the assistance of Borders Region Education Department, museum staff devised a series of activities to support specific **attainment outcomes** in Mathematics 5–14.

The influence of religion and the organisation of the church was very important in medieval Peebles. Pupils as monks could measure out scoops and grind down the volume of herbs to make herbal remedies. A group of children were given the task of designing and making a stained glass window for the Parish Church which was put in place before they left. Thus Mathematics was used in the context of design in order that the pupil might understand, use and apply concepts, facts and techniques associated with the properties of two and three dimensional objects. Differentiation (flexibility to allow for different abilities) could be achieved by adding criteria, for example: the range of shapes to be used could be stated; the design might have to be done to scale first on a smaller sheet of paper; the design might/might not have to be symmetrical.

ATTAINMENT OUTCOME	STRANDS
Number, money and measurement	● Measure and estimate
Shape, position and movement	● Range of shapes ● Symmetry

A similar type of activity involved pupils in creating a mosaic tiled floor for the rich person's house where the children had to find shapes which would fit together as tiles.

Many of the activities involved measuring, using non-standard measures such as hand spans or arm lengths, and weighing using balancing scales and a tron (weigh beam). As well as learning how to read scales, the pupils had to establish a standard measure for weighing bread using the tron. These activities allowed pupils to understand, use and apply concepts, facts and techniques in measurement. The medieval markets were an important interface between the residents of the town and those outside the boundaries. Country produce and raw materials were brought in and goods manufactured in the burgh were sold. The weight of the goods was strictly controlled, and harsh penalties were imposed for those using short weights. Pupils role-played both those selling and buying goods. If they were found to be short measuring they could be put in the stocks!

"I must be sure to give the correct measure!"

Religious and Moral Education 5–14

"As in other curricular areas, Religious and Moral Education can be taught in the context of a subject-based topic or theme. At other times it will contribute, along with other subjects, to a multidisciplinary approach, for example as part of an environmental studies topic in primary schools."

NATIONAL GUIDELINES, RELIGIOUS
AND MORAL EDUCATION, 5–14

Religion has played a major role in shaping the history, culture and identity of people for thousands of years. Religious Education fosters an appreciation of religion as an important expression of human experience. Pupils' own beliefs develop as they gain knowledge and understanding of Christianity and other world religions. Moral Education, which is conveyed through other aspects of the curriculum as well as religious education, contributes significantly to the personal and social development of pupils as they learn skills of moral judgement about what is considered right and wrong, self awareness, and how to relate to others in a multicultural society.

The National Guidelines divide Religious and Moral Education into three **attainment outcomes**:

- Christianity
- Other World Religions
- Personal Search.

Each of these can be supported by museums and their collections.

CHRISTIANITY

Blairs Museum, near Aberdeen, is dedicated to telling the history of the Catholic Church in Scotland through its displays and collections. Furthermore, many local museums have paintings and artefacts relating to Christianity, such as communion tokens, bibles, prayer books, chalices, communion plate and robes. These can show how Christianity has developed in the local community over a period of time, in some areas even creating new communities as in the towns which grew around the Border Abbeys.

OTHER WORLD RELIGIONS

In Glasgow, the St Mungo Museum of Religious Life and Art is an excellent resource for Christianity and Other World Religions. Here foreign ethnography, ie material culture from cultures other than our own, is intermingled with ethnographic and historical material from Britain and Europe in a truly multicultural way. This museum was the perfect setting for the exhibition, *The Chinese Way*, which used ethnographic materials to create opportunities for pupils to gain an understanding of the origins of certain aspects of Chinese Life, and to help them understand the value for Chinese people in maintaining their customs and traditions while living in this country. This exhibition focused on the Social Subjects component of Environmental Studies 5–14 and targeted classes, P5–7. However, the education content of the exhibition was in truth cross-curricular, and had strong links to Religious and Moral Education.

The Chinese dragon invites you to explore the Chinese way of life.

A large number of local museums in Scotland also hold foreign ethnographic collections. They are a valuable part of an area's local history, reflecting exploration, travel, trade, missionary activities and colonial interests. A lot of the belief systems of other cultures are incorporated in their material culture, such as the bark paintings of Aborigines, and the totem poles from North America. Other artefacts may represent faiths such as Buddhism, Hinduism, Islam, Judaism, Sikhism or Taoism. Moreover, there may be artefacts, particularly costume, which show how religion has become interwoven with many aspects of daily life, such as birth and marriage.

PERSONAL SEARCH

It has already been shown how a museum education project which focused on the preventive conservation of objects provided an opportunity to make pupils aware of environmental issues, such as pollution, relevant to contemporary society, thus developing the idea of human responsibility for present and future generations. Museum displays of natural history can provide similar opportunities, perhaps looking at endangered species. Examining fossils can lead to discussion of ideas about the creation of the world and the formulation of questions about it. Pupils can be made familiar with a number of different creation stories and myths from different cultures as they investigate objects from foreign ethnography collections. Moral dilemmas about the location and display of ethnographic material can be explored.

Expressive Arts: 5–14

Expressive Arts is the term used to include work in one or more of the following subject areas:

- Art and Design
- Drama
- Music
- Physical Education.

As their name suggests, the Expressive Arts place special emphasis on developing creativity, imagination and personal response in pupils. Museum collections provide a vast and diverse resource to support this area of the curriculum.

The National Guidelines set out three **attainment outcomes**, common to all subject areas, in which children should become competent. Learning in Expressive Arts should include:

- **using** materials, techniques, skills and media
- **expressing** feelings, ideas, thoughts and solutions
- **evaluating** and **appreciating.**

The guidelines emphasise the relationship between acquiring concepts and skills within each expressive arts subject and using these in wider contexts across the curriculum to *"bring learning to life and give a depth of understanding and relevance to the learner"*. This is spoken of as 'learning in' and 'learning through' the Expressive Arts. Many activities in museums involve both, often simultaneously.

Two projects within the Museums Education Initiative specifically focused on the Expressive Arts, the first concentrating on Drama, the second on Art and Design.

Case Study:
DRAMA
THE TRIAL OF CHRISTIAN MACDONALD AT THE CROMARTY COURTHOUSE

A study of artefacts from any historical period can help pupils to gain an understanding of the people who lived at that time. Role play of a historical event provides opportunities to heighten awareness and increase empathy for past societies ('learning through' Drama), while at the same time developing dramatic skills and techniques ('learning in' Drama). If these role play situations are enacted in the museum itself among the artefacts the benefits are greatly increased.

The Trial of Christian Macdonald is aimed at pupils aged nine to twelve, and forms part of a school visit to Cromarty Courthouse. It is based on a real case, tried in the Courthouse in 1841. The role play situation provides a variety of parts, from main roles to minor roles, to involve the whole class. These include: the accused, Christian Macdonald; the sheriff; the sheriff clerk; the procurator fiscal; a constable; fifteen members of the jury; the witnesses; and the public. It is enacted in costume, in the courtroom where the original trial took place and deals with many issues of the day. This particular trial was chosen because the verdict is unknown, giving the class the opportunity to reach their own verdict. The provision of such an activity which is open-ended engages pupils' imagination.

The visit to Cromarty Courthouse with the opportunity to re-enact the trial promotes: learning in a variety of integrated topics undertaken by primary schools, such as 'Victorians', 'Law and Order' or a local study; and specifically progression in learning for two of the **attainment outcomes** in Drama. Furthermore the source material which provided the original information is accessible for pupils studying history at Standard Grade.

ATTAINMENT OUTCOMES	STRANDS
Using materials, techniques, skills and media	● Investigating and experimenting ● Using movement and mime ● Using language
Expressing feelings, ideas, thoughts and solutions	● Communicating and presenting

The Trial of Christian Macdonald.

Case Study:

ART AND DESIGN
EARTH ART IN STRATHCLYDE

Museums present schools with many opportunities to help pupils take their learning in Art and Design further. Pupils are regularly asked to apply skills, such as the ability to observe and represent detail in order to record evidence from a variety of objects during museum visits. They may be asked to communicate their feelings, ideas and emotions in response to a display or an object. Collections of fine art and contemporary art exhibitions allow pupils to develop their capacity for evaluating and appreciating the work of artists and designers.

The project, *Earth Art*, was a collaborative venture undertaken by Paisley Museum and Art Gallery; Maclean Museum and Art Gallery, Greenock; and the Museum of Education, Scotland Street, Glasgow. It was inspired by the contemporary studio ceramics of Paisley Museum from which a touring exhibition of part of the collection was created, to be used as a teaching resource for critical studies in Art and Design within Expressive Arts 5–14.

The following table indicates the levels of skills and knowledge targeted during *Earth Art* with regard to appreciation of the work of the ceramic artists.

OUTCOME	STRANDS	LEVELS
Evaluating and appreciating	Observing, reflecting, describing and responding	**C** With support consider and discuss information from several sources, eg print, slide, video, catalogue. Using appropriate vocabulary make comparisons of art and design works. **D** Research information from supplied sources. Make a judgement about their own or another artist's work using appropriate vocabulary. Make a personal evaluation of own/others' designs, showing some understanding of design process. **E** Find out about an artist or designer and their work from several sources. Evaluate own design showing understanding of a design process, indicating modifications where appropriate.

Around the ceramics exhibition were built a series of outreach ceramics workshops involving local studio potters, during which pupils were able to progress in the remaining two **attainment outcomes**. These workshops were designed, not only to develop an effective link between the museum exhibition and classroom activity, but also to develop effective primary and secondary school liaison, in that primary school groups were invited to work in secondary school art departments.

Using materials, techniques, skills and media.
Expressing feelings, ideas, thoughts and solutions in the
Earth Art outreach workshops.

Personal and Social Development

"Personal and social development is a fundamental aspect of the education of the whole child and as such should permeate the whole curriculum. It is essentially concerned with the development of life skills...requiring pupils to increase their knowledge and understanding about themselves, others, their immediate environment and the world in which they live."

NATIONAL GUIDELINES,
PERSONAL AND SOCIAL
DEVELOPMENT 5–14

Two **outcomes** have been identified: **Personal Development** is essentially concerned with self-awareness and self-esteem; **Social Development** is concerned with inter-personal relationships, and independence and inter-dependence.

The methodology for teaching personal and social development lays particular emphasis on active or experiential learning which it indicates will only be effective if there is a climate of trust in which individuals and their personal experiences are listened to and accepted. The opportunities for experiential learning which museums provide grant **all** pupils the chance to learn and practise processes and skills which enable them to:

- look after their personal needs;
- work independently;
- participate effectively in groups;
- make their own decisions;
- assess their own abilities and capabilities.

The National Guidelines state that **all** pupils should have the opportunity to participate in and benefit from the full range of experiences offered in the area of personal and social development, including those with special educational needs. For *Let Me Show You!* the staff of the Hunterian Art Gallery, University of Glasgow, worked together to produce a project for children with all kinds of special needs.

Kelly-Anne from Richmond Park School in Glasgow

Case Study:

LET ME SHOW YOU
AN ART GALLERY PROJECT FOR CHILDREN WITH SPECIAL EDUCATIONAL NEEDS

In September 1993, the Education Officer of the Hunterian Art Gallery (a member of Strathclyde Region's Museum Education Service) devised a plan for a project for children from special schools. The theoretical basis for this project, contained in the unpublished document, *Let Me Show You!* (Anne Tynan, 1993) was drawn from the Museums & Galleries Commission's *Guidelines on Disability for Museums and Galleries in the United Kingdom* (1992), as well as from Strathclyde Regional Council's policy document on special educational needs, *Every Child is Special* (1993). The intention was to discover the extent to which it was possible to put the theory contained in these documents into practice.

AIMS OF THE PROJECT
The document *Let Me Show You!* states that the main aim of the project was *"to contribute to the quality of life of those with special needs"*. It was intended that the project should highlight ways in which all museums can work successfully with those with special needs, but this was not to be at the expense of the children involved.

Having stated this, the specific aims of the project included:

- to discriminate positively in favour of those children who have special educational needs, by means of a stimulating project which would enable creative self-expression;
- to help parents, pupils, teachers and the wider community to develop more positive attitudes to disadvantage and disability;
- to provide training for teachers in the use of museums and galleries by Special Needs groups, with particular reference to the curriculum National Guidelines;
- to provide training for the Gallery Education Officer and for other members of the Gallery staff in working with Special Needs groups; and
- to illustrate good practice in provision for Special Needs groups by museums and galleries.

PREPARATION
It was decided that *Let Me Show You!* would concentrate mainly on the Hunterian's 16th–17th-century paintings as it was felt that the subject matter of the paintings offered many possibilities for working with children with varying needs. Research into the paintings drew out information which would be appropriate to the groups involved. Artefacts relevant to the paintings were gathered together and costumes were selected from the Museum Education Service's costume collection, to be both handled and worn.

A list of special schools was obtained from Glasgow Division's Special Educational Needs Section. An initial mail-out about the project was made to 48 schools or units. Eight schools in categories ranging from moderate to profound learning difficulties showed an interest.

Between February and March 1994, a visit out to each school was made by the Education Officer, which was then followed by visits in to the Gallery by teachers from the schools. On the visits out, the Education Officer was able to meet the children likely to be involved in the project and to assess their needs. On the visits in to the Gallery, teachers were able to assess the building and the collections in terms of their children. On the basis of this dual assessment, a plan was made for each group of children, with dates for visits in to the Gallery being fixed.

Flexibility was given with regard to the number of visits made by groups and to the activities. The Education Officer was keen to have a high level of input from the teachers, who were well aware of the interests and abilities of their children.

VISITS IN BY SCHOOL GROUPS

Visits in to the Gallery took place over four months. Although there was great variety in the content of sessions, the activities could be divided into three main categories.

- Category One – Building and People Familiarisation
  This was important for all groups during their initial visit and for some groups, it was a feature of every visit. The 'familiarisation' ranged from touring around the main parts of the Gallery, to talking to the attendants on duty and exchanging first names. On a repeat visit, children would often return to features of the building which were pointed out previously, or would continue a conversation with a member of the Gallery staff. A characteristic of many children with special needs, regardless of their age and ability, is a lack of confidence. This 'familiarisation' gave the children a sense of belonging; this was now a safe environment, in which they could begin to focus on the collections.

- Category Two – Practical Activities
  The video of the project which was produced shows the range of practical activities carried out, both in the Gallery and back at school. In addition to the straightforward 'art' type activities – drawing, using pastels or plasticine, etc – groups produced costumes relating to the paintings; various friezes, with themes taken from the paintings; and even reproductions of the paintings, with reproduction gilded frames. One school used the sessions to explore medieval music, culminating with the children carrying out a medieval dance in wheelchairs in the midst of the Gallery. For those children with profound learning difficulties, staff used objects relating to the paintings to extend the type of 'hands-on' work at which special schools excel. Each child was helped to touch an object, which could be the focus of attention for a considerable length of time.

- Category Three – Exploring Behind the Scenes
  On some occasions, it was possible to take small groups of children into the 'hidden' parts of the Gallery, such as the offices and workshops, to meet the 'hidden staff' – the director, curators, office, technical and cleaning staff. This ongoing interchange meant that staff were able to follow the project in a way which would not normally have been possible; it also meant that children were able to see the Gallery and the collections in a new light.

CROSS-SESSIONAL WORK: 'GIVE ME A GROUP OF TEENAGERS...'

Special mention should be made of the work carried out by a small group of teenagers from one of the schools. One of the original ideas behind the project was that some of the more able children with special needs would be able to use their own experiences to enrich the visits of other less able children. The group of eight teenagers were able to do this in varying ways. Their principal task was to video the other groups during their sessions. The Education Officer gave the boys who carried out the filming full responsibility for their equipment and also for what they did with it. The two girls preferred to model the costumes and to help the other children to put them on.

Inevitably, the teenagers were drawn into the sessions – although they were always given the opportunity to withdraw if they found a situation too difficult. It was noticeable that on no occasion did this happen; even when an autistic child began to exhibit the first signs of a tantrum, the older boy remained perfectly calm and followed precisely instructions given to him. In this work with the teenagers, the Gallery's attendants were of crucial importance, reinforcing the teenagers' feelings of being 'accepted'.

BRINGING PARENTS AND THE PUBLIC INTO THE PROJECT

One of the aims of the project was: *"to help parents...and the wider community to develop more positive attitudes to disadvantage and disability"*.

Margaret-Clare O'Brien from St. Kevin's School, Glasgow

An exhibition about the project was mounted in the Gallery, in the midst of the paintings which had been the main focus for work. As well as enabling parents to share in their children's experiences, this was also another opportunity to increase the confidence of the children by putting their work on display next to the work of artists such as Rembrandt and Rubens.

Included in the exhibition were a range of artistic works, both individual and in the form of friezes, as well as some of the children's written work. Introductory panels gave information about the project, setting it in context, and text about each school was included beside the work of that school. As some children had not actually produced any external work, due to the severity of their conditions, photographs of them were displayed. Adjacent to the exhibition, a 20-minute video filmed by the teenagers was shown continuously throughout the six days of the exhibition, allowing the public to share in the atmosphere of the project.

The Education Officer remained in the Gallery throughout the exhibition, so as to be able to meet parents and to observe public reaction.

WHAT DID *LET ME SHOW YOU!* REALLY SHOW US?

More than with any other kind of educational work which is carried out in museums and galleries, one has to be very wary of looking for tangible results and 'successes' when one is working with children with special educational needs. Those who have profound learning difficulties will often display no external reaction or their reactions will become apparent only when one is familiar with them as individuals. With other children, activities such as chatting, talking to other staff, and examining parts of the building may not appear to have a deep educational content at first glance, until it is realised that more extensive educational work can only be carried out when the child feels that *"this is an atmosphere in which I am accepted as I am, with my own specific needs"*.

The following comments were among those received during an evaluation of the project in either a oral or a written form from the different schools.

"The initial appeal for our staff was the assurance that any involvement with the project would be pupil led...so a big attraction of the project was that it would go a long way to restoring lost confidence and self-esteem."

"An exploration of new indoor and outdoor environments was undertaken...an all-round sensory investigation was carried out where seeing, listening, talking and creative skills were all fully employed..."

"They worked publicly, which again helped their confidence and they were pleased when visitors and university staff took an interest in their work."

"They also benefited from working beside pupils from other schools, sharing in a social experience and developing social skills."

"I was certain that...would drop out but he thrived and grew with the experience. His tendency to show off was well channelled in the 'dressing up' sessions. He revelled in those. Having been excluded from five secondary schools because of unacceptable behaviour, this project completely caught his imagination. In feedback to staff he articulated very well how worthwhile and maturing an experience it had been for him. He had previously thought it impossible for him to work with children with disabilities, so he learned a great deal about himself."

"Featuring in the video was an added bonus which again made the pupils feel that their work was valued."

The most difficult type of evaluation is self-evaluation, which is an aspect of the *Let Me Show You!* evaluation which Gallery staff themselves must carry out. The project plan looked to raise the awareness of the staff and *"to develop more positive attitudes to disadvantage and disability"*.

Most staff agreed that their attitude towards people with disabilities had changed since taking part in the project, although there was also general agreement that they had not gained very much knowledge about specific disabilities.

With regard to their own attitudes and feelings about the project, staff commented:

"I think that I am now less worried about offending people with disabilities."

"The pupils' visits helped to raise the awareness of other staff of the abilities of pupils with multiple educational needs."

"I also think that the children enjoyed the cheeky banter of some staff, and responded likewise in a more confident manner than they might do normally. I think they saw the staff as 'adult friends' and not patronising, pitying onlookers."

CONCLUSIONS

It could be claimed that the museum world is the ideal starting point for a widespread programme for the promotion of the understanding of disability. Reasons for this are as follows:

- One of the core functions of museums is the promotion of the understanding of other human beings, through the understanding of their culture, their history, their social environment, their inventions etc. This understanding should be a living understanding. A visitor with a disability should feel that through its staff, the museum is also interested in him/her, is aware of any possible problems and will react sympathetically in any difficulties.
- This 'living understanding' should hopefully be found in the majority of other museum visitors, who will have come to the museum for a variety of reasons but mainly reasons connected to their desire to learn.
- Museums provide a 'protected' environment. The protection provided for the collections, particularly in the form of those who act as attendants or warders, is also available for the visitor, who (hopefully) is able to relax in the knowledge that he or she is in a 'safe' environment. This protection is also reassuring for those who accompany visitors with certain needs which at certain moments, may necessitate direct intervention on the part of staff, eg in situations where an older child or adult who is autistic may display violent behaviour.
- Through their collections, museums provide a rich resource of interests, which can engage the attention of people of all levels. They provide an enriching environment which can offer stimulation and cultural development.

It is hoped that anyone reading this case study will have gained some insight into what the museum world should be able to achieve in working with visitors with disabilities. However, it should not be forgotten that there is absolutely no substitute for personal contact, as this is the only true means by which one can come to an understanding of what museums can offer for those with disabilities.

Anne Tynan
June 1995
Anne Tynan was Education Officer at the Hunterian Museum and Art Gallery at the time of this project which has been shortlisted for the 1995 Gulbenkian Award for the Most Imaginative Education Work. She has since become Special Educational Needs Co-ordinator at the Science Museum in London where she is continuing to develop this work.

Developing Skills for Life-long Learning

...in the 5–14 curriculum

The value of a museum visit in the development of personal and interpersonal skills has been clearly recognised as pupils interact with their peers, museum staff, and other visitors during a visit. Furthermore, this publication shows how working with museum collections provides opportunities to develop imagination, creativity, and language skills in talking, listening, reading and writing which are fundamental to life-long learning. Another important aspect of museum education is its ability to assist in the development of the skills of enquiry and investigation which enable us to gather and process information in order to gain knowledge and understanding, and develop informed attitudes about the world in which we live.

As part of the Museums Education Initiative, Fife Museums Forum worked with a variety of classes studying different topics in local schools to produce the video, *A Class of Their Own: the museum as a learning resource*. This video is aimed at both teachers and museum staff, and seeks to encourage greater and more effective use of museums by schools, particularly in the development of skills for life-long learning. Moreover, it illustrates how the 5–14 curriculum actively promotes the development of investigative learning skills through its framework of **strands** in Environmental Studies 5–14. In museums those skills are strengthened as pupils learn to use objects as evidence to support a line of enquiry in their classroom study.

In order to follow and draw conclusions from that enquiry, pupils must first learn how to plan their study. Making decisions about what they need to find out during their visit to the museum, determining the sources of evidence available to them and what kinds of questions will elicit the required information, and practising accurate observing, describing and visual recording of objects, are all valuable pre-visit learning activities.

"Now how do I do this?"

Such skills, practised in class, will be further reinforced in the museum, and will yield a wealth of information about the objects on display. Some questions may be straight forward and easily answered involving reference only to the object's physical features as seen at that moment in time: what is it made of?; and what is its shape, colour, size and texture? Other questions may require some hypothesising or deduction as pupils look for clues, sometimes obtained only from fragments of the original object, and speculate as to how it was made, what it was used for, who might have used it and when. In doing so they can begin to compare and contrast important features of different times and places. Working in groups, pupils should be invited to voice their opinions based on their interpretation of the evidence before them, rather than be expected to give the 'right' answer. Thus the evidence is discussed and evaluated, allowing pupils to reach their own conclusions to inform their study or to highlight the need for further research back in the classroom.

Different methods used to record collected evidence on site can assist in developing skills in writing, drawing, tape or video recording, and photography. Pupils can draw or sketch what they observe, make lists and pictorial charts, take a sequence of photographs, make annotated diagrams, take notes, tape-record their own impressions or an interview with the curator. Information-handling skills may be enhanced as pupils learn how to classify objects according to a variety of criteria and record that information in manageable way as tables, graphs or time-lines. In the museum, individuals or groups of pupils may be asked to report on their findings to the whole class, drawing their attention to the appropriate object or objects as sources of evidence, while back in the classroom a whole range of presentation skills can be developed as a result of the visit, allowing for progression in learning in language and the expressive arts.

ENVIRONMENTAL STUDIES 5–14 – COMPONENTS: SOCIAL SUBJECTS, SCIENCE AND TECHNOLOGY

STRANDS	SKILLS WHICH CAN BE DEVELOPED THROUGH WORKING WITH MUSEUM OBJECTS
Planning	Identifying sources Identifying questions Practising looking and describing
Collecting Evidence	Observing Listening Questioning Describing Sorting/Classifying Sequencing Discussing
Recording and Presenting	Writing Drawing Tape-recording Video-recording Taking photographs Information handling Reporting findings orally Displaying findings visually Presenting through role-play/drama
Interpreting and Evaluating	Assessing design/technology of objects Speculating on fragmentary evidence Making deductions from evidence
Developing Informed Attitudes	Distinguishing between fact and opinion Empathising with other people/societies

Environmental Studies 5–14, therefore, encourages the progressive development, during primary school and the first two years of secondary education, of the investigative skills and strategies which are so much at the heart of life-long learning. These are currently further developed in the secondary school beyond the age of 14 by pupils studying Standard Grade, Revised Higher and Certificate of Sixth Year Study (CSYS) courses as pupils assume more responsibility for their own learning.

...in Standard Grade Arrangements

Students in years S3 and S4 of secondary schools are engaged in a curriculum which follows certain guiding principles approved by the Secretary of State for Scotland and issued in the form of guidelines from the Scottish Consultative Council on the Curriculum. These state that the various courses, and short or modular courses, should give adequate experience of all the following eight 'modes' of study which formed the curriculum in the first two years of secondary schooling, and which continue into the third and later years:

- Language and Communication
- Mathematical Studies and Applications
- Scientific Studies and Applications
- Social and Environmental Studies
- Technical Activities and Applications
- Creative and Aesthetic Activities
- Physical Education
- Religious and Moral Education

It is generally agreed that all pupils between 12 and 16 should study at least one course related to each mode. For most modes there are several subjects and courses to choose from. S3 and S4 pupils take a number of two-year Standard Grade courses and may also take Scottish Examination Board (SEB) short courses and SCOTVEC modules which are seen as a flexible means of promoting breadth and balance in the curriculum. In Standard Grade courses, pupils are assessed against performance criteria related to three levels of award from the SEB, at Foundation, General and Credit, thus suiting every level of ability.

During primary school years and the first two years of secondary education, pupils generally visit museums in groups as part of a whole class study. By the time they reach Standard Grade it is likely that pupils will be looking to museums for assistance with individual study. A number of the main modes include an investigation element and there are opportunities for pupils to carry this element into the museum dimension as they research information, building on the skills practised during earlier years of investigating collections. Moreover, staff development materials for Standard Grade list the use of museums and other resources outwith the school as 'Indicators of Good Practice' in Science, Art & Design, Contemporary Social Studies, Biology, Geography, History, Modern Studies, and Home Economics.

How 5–14 articulates with Standard Grade has been a major concern in secondary schools, but there is no doubt of continued progression in the development of the skills required for life-long learning.

"The development of skills provides a means of progression in studying history. Pupils will have had experience of many of the skills being developed in this course at earlier stages in their study of history; the skills will also be developed further at later stages."

STANDARD GRADE, AMENDED
ARRANGEMENTS IN HISTORY
(SEB 1993)

The 5-14 documents state precise linkages in relevant subjects between the framework of strands and Standard Grade requirements. An example of continuity in the development of investigative skills is taken from the National Guidelines Environmental Studies 5–14, Social Subjects:

STRANDS	SKILLS WHICH CAN BE DEVELOPED THROUGH WORKING WITH MUSEUM OBJECTS
Planning	Plan an investigation by suggesting aims, explaining methods of enquiry, devising questions to structure the investigation and indicating sources.
Collecting Evidence	Continue to extend their awareness of the range of possible sources of evidence; identify sources appropriate to an enquiry; use appropriate methods to extract and record relevant information from a range of sources.
Recording and Presenting	Communicate clearly the main findings and valid conclusions of an enquiry, based on relevant evidence.
Interpreting and Evaluating	Select appropriate techniques to process and interpret information; demonstrate the ability to draw and justify conclusions; identify, express and evaluate points of view; explain the importance of events in an historical context; evaluate reliability, bias, objectivity of evidence; engage in informed debate; apply knowledge and show empathy with people living in other periods and other locations.

Pupils are often encouraged to choose issues for investigation of a local and precise nature, which is where the collections of authentic pictorial, written and three-dimensional primary source material in local museums can be of great value. Falkirk Museums Service History Research Centre, at Callendar House, provides information on and access to all the collections held by Falkirk Museums and is a major centre for historical research on Falkirk District. Its resources include: archives on local businesses, people, societies, and organisations; photographs depicting the way of life of the people of Falkirk District; maps and plans; information surveys; films and videos; sound archives of local people and a small reference library to assist Standard Grade pupils independently investigating the social, industrial and natural history of the area.

As with the provision of resources to support the 5–14 curriculum, teachers and museum staff should work together to identify source material available within the museum to support these investigations. If teachers are aware of the strengths of the collections of local museums they can ensure that pupils too are aware of those strengths at the outset when they are choosing issues for investigation. Similarly, if museums investigate what topics are specified as being general areas for investigation, they can be clear about what they are able to offer, even to the extent of putting together resource packs for particular topics, with sub-divisions on issues for which there is appropriate source material. These resource packs can hold two types of material: that which is specific to the local area; and that of a more generic nature which widens the appeal of the pack to schools outwith the immediate area. Teachers can contribute to these resource packs in the compilation of a bibliography of suggested reading.

Many museum services are producing resource packs, primarily to support Standard Grade History investigations. Among these are:

- Strathclyde Regional Archives, where the Museums Education Service is closely involved with the Education Development Service (Glasgow Division) and has produced a number of historical publications based on the resources at the Archives.
- Edinburgh City Museums and Galleries, where resource packs have been produced which link the displays of The People's Story Museum to suggested issues for investigation and provide extracts from historical sources.
- New Lanark World Heritage Village, where the Standard Grade resource pack, *Investigating New Lanark, 1785–1990*, was produced and subsequently distributed by Scottish CCC to every secondary school in Scotland.
- The Scottish Mining Museum, where successful collaboration between teachers and museums generated *Coal Mining in the Lothians*, part of Lothian Region Education Department's series of Standard Grade History Archives, *Footprints Through Time*. The Scottish Mining Museum, Lady Victoria Colliery, Newtongrange, has an extensive library and archive collection from which two local teachers were able to select appropriate material to support a number of suggested issues for investigation, as well as to provide suggestions for fieldwork activities at the colliery.

GUIDELINES FOR MUSEUM STAFF PRODUCING RESOURCE PACKS FOR STANDARD GRADE HISTORY

Preliminary work
- Make contact with the local education authority/local teachers to establish the range of topics from which issues for investigation might arise.
- Assess the museum's collections to establish which topics the museum can support.
- Invite teachers to write an introduction, a list of suggested issues for investigation, and prepare a bibliography for each topic.

Identifying source material
- Select a variety of material, both pictorial and written, to stimulate pupils' interest: photographs; drawings; maps; prints; letters; newspaper reports; statistics; charts; advertisements; reports; minutes of meetings etc. Recordings of appropriate reminiscence sessions with elderly people can be included, along with a transcript.

- Include recommendations for fieldwork activities at the museum for pupils wishing to use additional source material: links made to museum displays; attention drawn to particular objects, some of which may be handled; invitations to interview members of the museum staff where appropriate. Pupils may wish to use cameras or tape-recorders during fieldwork activities.

Collating and presenting the source material

- Sub-divide topics into manageable parts for which the museum can provide appropriate source material, eg housing: overcrowding; sanitation; rents; slum clearance etc.
- Obtain copyright clearance before replicating sources and include acknowledgements within the pack where this is requested.
- Ensure that material included in the pack is of high quality as pupils may wish to photocopy sources for their own use.
- Transcribe extracts from documents when the original is of poor quality or difficult to read, but include a photocopy of the original as well as the transcription within the archive so that pupils can see what the original document looked like.
- Cross-reference written and pictorial source material.
- Bear in mind the different levels of ability of Standard Grade pupils and include source material of varying complexity to allow for differentiation. Seek advice and guidance in this area from Learning Support staff in schools. An explanation of the meaning of difficult of unfamiliar words should also be included, either with the source or in a glossary.

Marketing the packs

- Work with the Local Authority Education Resource Centres who can often give assistance with the marketing and distribution of packs. It is worth noting that packs produced in collaboration with local teachers will have greater credibility with other teachers.
- Establish set times when curatorial staff will be available to assist pupils with their investigation, answer questions, or give interviews.

...and in the Post-16 Curriculum: Higher Still

The most recent in the series of reforms of the Scottish education system was announced in March 1994 in *Higher Still: Opportunity for All*, the document outlining the government's proposals for the reform of upper secondary education in Scotland.

"The goal of Higher Still is to provide opportunity for all students to reach the highest standards of which they are capable across a broad range of subjects and to develop competence in the core skills of communication, numeracy, problem solving, information technology and personal and interpersonal skills. In this way, they will be prepared to play a full part in a rapidly changing society."

HIGHER STILL, CONSULTATION
DOCUMENT, AUTUMN 1995

This response to the recommendations of the Howie Committee intends that the reforms should build on recent developments, namely the introduction of Standard Grade and the associated revision of Highers and Certificate of Sixth Year Studies (CSYS) courses, SCOTVEC's National Certificate modules and the grouping of these into general Scottish Vocational Qualifications (gSVQs). The main task is to link existing SEB and SCOTVEC provision into one unified and coherent framework, allowing appropriate progression in S5 and S6 for students of all levels of prior attainment.

The Higher Still framework of Units, Courses and National Certificates is currently at the consultation stage. The aim is to ensure that courses and units are available at the right level in the desired range of subjects, and lead to recognised qualifications. A draft format for course and unit documents has been devised, drawing on the best features of current SEB arrangements documents and SCOTVEC descriptors. A range of National Certificates will also be available, comprising specified combinations of courses and/or units from the specialist frameworks. Students will be free to choose whether to follow a free-standing programme of courses and units or a programme leading to a National Certificate.

The curriculum and assessment system of Higher Still places great emphasis on the development of skills which are divided into:

- learning and study skills;
- the core skills of communication, numeracy, problem solving, personal and interpersonal skills, and information technology;
- specialist skills, reflecting students needs and aspirations.

Certification of the five core skills is being advocated, reflecting that in a rapidly changing world, competence in the core skills is essential as a foundation for life-long personal development. Although learning and study skills will not be certificated, they are recognised as being of fundamental importance and their development should be a priority in learning and teaching approaches.

Within the general principles for the post-16 curriculum the Rationale states that:

"The individual can benefit in all aspects of life from a capability for life-long learning and development. A post-16 curriculum should therefore be based on a set of aims which emphasise the development of personal qualities and the skills, knowledge and understanding which support personal and social development as well as more specialised knowledge and skills."

PRINCIPLES FOR THE POST-16
CURRICULUM (SCOTTISH CCC,
APRIL 1995)

The principles for the post-16 curriculum are consistent with those of the 5–14 curriculum and Standard Grade. Furthermore they not only actively promote continued progression in the development of personal qualities, skills, and knowledge and understanding, but state that students are **entitled** to be offered a range of experiences which contribute to that development. Having established the significant contribution of museum education in the earlier stages of the education system in Scotland, opportunities for the continued use of museums into the upper secondary school should be explored by teachers and museum staff together. Such exploration can lead to innovative ways of museums and schools working together for their mutual benefit.

Opportunities for museums and schools to help each other are more numerous than might be imagined. Museums can provide a 'real-life' opportunity for pupils studying for Higher examinations to contribute to the development of a museum. Such opportunities arise in areas such as Higher Management and Information Studies where the investigation element of the course might allow pupils to investigate a museum's marketing strategy to schools, tourists or other visitors. Students of Art and Design can access a rich variety of visual material to stimulate expressive and design studies. Opportunities exist to promote a museum through photography, video and graphic design. Foreign language students might like to try producing text in their chosen language for a welcoming leaflet or audiotape aimed at a museum's overseas visitors.

An innovative opportunity to involve students of Higher Computer Studies in the development of the local museum arose in Ullapool, and was developed as part of the Museums Education Initiative.

Case Study:

HIGHER COMPUTER STUDIES
ULLAPOOL MUSEUM IN PARTNERSHIP WITH ULLAPOOL HIGH SCHOOL

Ullapool Museum is a small independent museum trust which until recently was run entirely by volunteers drawn from the local community. The Board of Trustees appointed their first full-time curator in Autumn 1995 on the re-opening of the museum building which had been closed for a year whilst undergoing complete refurbishment. Ullapool Museum has developed a good relationship with local schools, but acknowledges that its remote geographical location places extra restrictions on teachers further afield becoming familiar with its collections.

Ullapool High School student investigating database applications for use by the local museum.

BACKGROUND TO THE PROJECT

The strength of Ullapool Museum is its written and pictorial evidence of the life and times, and the migration, of the people of Wester Ross going back over many generations. Working in collaboration with the teacher of Computer Studies at Ullapool High School, and students undertaking the SEB Higher examination, four separate investigations were identified which together would provide a feasibility study for the museum with regard to the use of information technology to enhance public access to its archives, and increase their availability to other museums and schools.

The long-term aim, when the idea originated, was to create a genealogical database using source material available from museum archives and public records, the intention being for the museum to hold the parent database, a programme called 'Brother's Keeper' capable of holding genealogical information of one million names. Other small programmes of varying complexity would be produced for use by schools for data collection and analysis. The ultimate desire was to encourage as much cross-curricular activity as possible from as many age groups through their investigation of simple records of names, birth, christening, marriage, death and burial dates, lineage charts, register charts, relationship diagrams, descendancy charts, time-line reports. This would give other teachers in remote sites opportunities to use the resources, thus the museum could undertake a proactive role in curriculum support and facilitate development of learning skills through inquiry and investigation.

THE INVESTIGATIONS

The immediate task was to investigate how to integrate the gathering of family history with modern technology in order to create a genealogical database. Two investigations dealt with this problem, whilst the remaining two dealt with the possibility of creating a multi-media programme which would enhance and give remote access to the collections of Ullapool Museum.

Student 1 investigated the 'Brother's Keeper' database to see if files could be merged, allowing several people to work on the database and join up their files to make one large database (collaborative databasing). This student also produced a manual to ensure that the coding terminology would be consistent over the different groups.

Student 2 investigated whether the 'Brothers Keeper' database could be accessed remotely, and subsequently looked at the cost implications and technology required.

Student 3 investigated how to gather multimedia data and looked into the different methods of capturing images.

Student 4 investigated the different formats of CD's, and how to put the images created by Student 3 into a multimedia presentation.

WHAT DID THIS PROJECT DO

...for the students:

- One of the main benefits to the students was that they investigated a 'real-life' situation for examination purposes, working within a real museum's development programme, and in doing so gained an insight into aspects of computing and its application they might never otherwise have ventured.
- They gained experience of working collaboratively with museums and other organisations, such as the Regional Archivist at Inverness.

- Although the investigations were individual pieces of work, the students gained experience of working in a team as one investigation supported the other.
- They were able to confidently present their findings to members of Ullapool Museum's Board of Trustees.
- Those students carrying on with CSYS Computing Studies are already focused on stated goals.

...for the museum:

- It raised awareness about the use of information technology to enhance displays and provide access to underused parts of the collection. As the museum was until recently run and maintained by volunteers it was necessary to support and encourage members to become involved with the development of information technology.
- It provided access to skills, knowledge and equipment which the museum did not have.
- The results of these investigations will enable Ullapool Museum to make informed decisions about how it wants to proceed, particularly as the investigations looked at the cost implications for different methods of access.
- It now has a concise but complete user guide to data entry for the genealogical database, and a realistic expectation of the level of input required to create it.
- Interest is running high at the possibility of producing a multimedia presentation. Two of the four students are now taking CSYS Computer Studies and are keen to take their multimedia projects further. Jointly they are to make up, and put onto CD, a 'walkthrough' of the school and, having learned from this, hope to work together with the museum on a multimedia presentation for the museum.
- It provided an opportunity for Ullapool Museum to improve the quality of its links with the local High School.

...for the school:

- The school received the Toyota Award for Science and Industry in recognition of the innovative nature of the project. This enabled the Computer Studies Department to buy equipment they would have otherwise been unable to afford.
- Working in partnership with Ullapool Museum on the next stage of the project will give them access to further funding.
- The school will ultimately be able to use the completed database and multimedia presentation to support other curricular modes.

...for Higher Still:

- Higher Still gives increasing importance to the development of information technology skills, reflecting its growing influence in our lives. The Museums Education Initiative project carried out at Ullapool illustrates another area where its use is becoming more widespread. Thematic multimedia programmes on CD-ROM, giving access to the immense resource capabilities of museums are already being produced, and as technology advances museums are now contemplating the move from information pack to World Wide Web.

Part 3
UPFRONT:
choosing the appropriate strategy

The Museums Education Initiative was concerned to support pilot projects which not only addressed different areas of the curriculum but also illustrated the variety of approaches to making collections accessible to a young audience. Education provision for schools can take many forms but generally falls into one of two categories:

- direct teaching
- resource provision.

Direct teaching has traditionally included such activities as themed guided tours and object handling sessions which are generally undertaken on both a proactive and reactive basis by members of the museum staff. Other activities, such as workshops, demonstrations, role-play and drama sessions often require additional help from skilled demonstrators or teachers and are usually linked to a specific exhibition. The common denominator in all of these activities is that they are very labour intensive and require a huge commitment in terms of time from museum staff. Many museums, unable to commit as much time as they would wish to school groups, are changing the emphasis of some of their direct teaching activities from pupils to teachers. Through the provision of in-service courses or teachers' awareness raising sessions, they are seeking to empower teachers to work effectively in the museum with their own pupils. In this way museums endeavour to reach a greater number of children.

Resource provision has included exhibitions and displays, which may be supplemented by a range of written materials: teachers' information/resource packs; activity sheets; and pupil project packs such as those prepared for Standard Grade pupils. It may also include outreach provision in the form of a loans service or mobile museum. The initial cost of producing such resources may be high and will almost certainly require an intensive input of time from museum staff, but having once been produced the emphasis is long-term and independent use by teachers and pupils. Problems which do arise tend to be with maintenance and administration of the resources.

A museum education service will ideally provide a combination of direct teaching and resource provision, but the balance between the two will depend very much on the resources of the museum itself: its collections; space, facilities and equipment for educational use; the skills and experience of staff and others in the community available for education work; and how much money is available.

"Are you having a nice time?"
...direct teaching at the National Galleries
of Scotland

Visitors to the National Galleries of Scotland will hear Michael Cassin ask this question of all school groups who come to the National Galleries to 'look at' the paintings. From the laughter and obvious enjoyment of the pupils, they might be fooled into thinking that *"having a nice time"* is all that is taking place. This is far from being the case.

There is a kind of magic in the way Michael Cassin encourages school groups to interact with the paintings, and he certainly uses a few tricks. These tricks are part of a carefully structured approach which is designed to promote the optimum amount of learning. The real magic though is in the paintings, and the aim of the staff in the Education Department of the National Galleries is to help children to gain confidence in interpreting paintings, and to derive enjoyment in so doing, in order that they will want to come back to explore the galleries further and look at other paintings.

"The one advantage galleries and museums have over anywhere else is that they contain collections of objects and images which may be beautiful, interesting, amusing, exciting, stimulating, or in some way special. The one thing which you can do in a museum that you can't do anywhere else is to explore original works face-to face, and the specialness of this experience is as worthy of preservation as the collections themselves."

MICHAEL CASSIN

At the National Galleries the emphasis is totally on the paintings. Whatever the topic or subject area there will be paintings to support them.

A group of children studying the Jacobites had come to visit the Dynasty exhibition at the National Portrait Gallery in Edinburgh. Just how much would a group of 10-and 11-year-olds get out of looking at a series of portraits, one might wonder. The first 'trick' was to get the attention of all the children. *"This is the skull of Robert Bruce."* Now who wouldn't be impressed with that! There was a reason to begin with the skull of course, apart from the fact that children love anything gory. It provided the starting point to talk about the Stewart family and how they got their name. Intrigued, the children were eager to move on to the first painting to find out more about this family.

Initially they were reticent and had to be given lots of prompts to search out the evidence in the paintings which told them as much about the political intrigue of that time as it did about each family member. Thus they were introduced to the idea that historical paintings were often used for propaganda purposes and as such had a more complex story to tell. They were always encouraged to look and keep looking until they found the clues. *"...as if by magic."* If it was a difficult clue to interpret the children were *"...let into a secret"* which was whispered to them as they hung on every word. By the time the children were looking at the third painting they had got the idea and were brimming with ideas, suggestions and opinions, all of which were taken seriously even if they were *"brilliant...completely wrong...but brilliant"*. The paintings were carefully selected in that the same clues were repeated in different portraits, thus reinforcing and building on knowledge and understanding. Moreover, the children became excited and quite proud of themselves as they recognised each clue.

At the end of the session the class teacher showed amazement that the group had become so involved with the paintings. One boy remarked on how much he had enjoyed it and that it wasn't what he expected:

"What did you expect?" asked Michael Cassin of the children.

"I thought it would be boring," was one reply.

"A lecture," said another. *"I thought you would stand up and tell us who painted the picture, when it was painted and things like that."*

"Is that what you want?" asked Michael, *"I can do that."*

"No" said all the children together. *"Keep it like it is."*

They obviously had a *"nice time"*!

Michael Cassin empowering children to interpret paintings in the National Galleries of Scotland.

SUMMARY POINTS:

DO...

- use or adapt this kind of approach in ways which suit your own personality to do something equally appropriate with your own collections in your museum or gallery.
- your research. It is important to know your subject, know your collections, and know your audience.
- make links between artefacts and build on those links as you go round, constantly referring to them and reminding pupils about them.
- start with an attention-grabber, eg "This is the biggest painting in Scotland". Any artefact can become an attention-grabber by finding something interesting/unusual to say about it. Start with the one near the door, or just round the corner.
- get to know the children, asking who they are whenever they answer a question or offer an opinion. Remember their names and use them. If you forget apologise - let them know you're interested in them.
- talk to the people on the edges. Be a sheepdog and draw them in.
- be a performer and use who you are: your height; your voice, varying the tempo and volume; gestures.
- encourage children to look for the clues. Start off with lots of prompts, encourage opinions, repeat answers so that the whole class can hear them. Even if the answers are wrong, take them seriously. Build up confidence.

DO NOT...

- give a lecture. This approach is all about empowerment, giving the children the feeling they can do it for themselves.

An Artist in Residence Workshop at the Talbot Rice Gallery

The Talbot Rice Gallery, part of Edinburgh University, is one of the leading venues for the presentation of contemporary art. The exhibition *Changing Places* featured paintings, sculpture and drawings by Margaret Hunter. The artist, originally from Glasgow, now lives and works in Berlin for part of each year. During her time in Germany she has seen great political and social changes, and it is these experiences of conflict and division which act as a stimulus for her paintings and sculpture.

The idea to develop a project for school groups came from the gallery. Margaret was available to be 'in residence' for a week at the start of the month-long exhibition. The opportunity to offer pupils the experience working with a leading Scottish contemporary artist was extremely inviting. The emphasis was on using a workshop approach to provide access to and understanding of the work of the artist, and to use 'art' as a means of expressing how we feel and communicating these feelings to others.

Three schools in Lothian Region took part, involving a range of classes from P2 to P7. As an in-built part of the project a member of the project team visited each school and spoke to the class teachers. This was extremely valuable in assessing the levels at which to pitch each workshop. Teachers were asked to prepare their classes both through a variety of pre-visit activities, and in practical ways, such as ensuring that the classes were split into four groups to save time in a tight

Margaret Hunter surrounded by her own work and the children's work it inspired.

schedule at the gallery. Post-evaluation was also discussed at this time. The purpose of these visits was to integrate the Gallery experience with classroom study.

Preparation in the Gallery started with a planning meeting between the artist and the four adult helpers which enabled a strategy for the week to be drawn up to fit the timetable. It also ensured that everyone was familiar with the proposed structure for the workshops, and their role within in it. The layout of workstations to accommodate four groups of children had to be decided on, while materials had to be gathered and distributed amongst the four work areas.

THE WORKSHOP

The workshop, which lasted one and a half hours, was structured in three parts:

- introduction
- practical activity
- question time.

The artist introduced the exhibition and drew the children's attention to the way she communicated her feelings through facial expressions and gestures, and the colours and textures she used.

The aim of the practical activity was for the pupils to make a mask which communicated their ideas and feelings. They were asked to choose an emotion for their mask – sad, happy, fierce etc.– and to think about the colours and kinds of lines and marks which would best express the emotion. They worked on the Gallery floor with the artist's work all around them. The stylisation of her work, influenced by 'primitive' art and its likeness to children's art made the exhibition an ideal setting for a mask-making project. Materials and approaches altered to accommodate each individual class. The finished artwork was displayed at the Gallery and returned to the schools during follow-up visits.

"Time was limited and it was important to get into the practical work as quickly as possible. The tight schedule was a worry on the first day, but it was astonishing how quickly the children concentrated, first drawing their ideas on rolls of white paper which we had laid out on the floor. One of the main aspects of the project was that the children should have the freedom to express their own ideas and that the choices should be theirs. Our job was to provide a variety of materials, advise on techniques and to give encouragement.

After the work was completed, what turned out to be one of the most important parts of the workshop was to go up to the balcony of the gallery so that the children could survey their work which had been lined up below. After the practical work and concentration the children felt pleased and justifiably proud of their masks. They noticed that the ideas and strong colours did not look so very different from my work hanging on the walls and at this stage they could identify with me and felt themselves also as artists. This was the time when the children felt happy and relaxed enough to ask questions.

At the end of a tiring but satisfying week, which was a kind of highlight for me during my exhibition at the Talbot Rice Gallery, I felt elated by the wonderful, inventive work which the children had produced and at their response to my exhibition."

MARGARET HUNTER, ARTIST IN
RESIDENCE

SUMMARY POINTS:

DO...

- wherever possible carry out workshops in the gallery or alongside the exhibition which inspired the workshop. It may be more practical and convenient to hold potentially messy workshops in a separate room, but the educational impact of the original work is very much reduced.
- prepare thoroughly to ensure the smooth running of a workshop. Planning meetings should involve all workshop leaders who should be allocated specific operational tasks (eg to collect in and wash all paint/glue brushes ready for the next session), as well as general duties (eg to work with group 1 on workstation A).
- take care to integrate the gallery experience with work going on in the classroom. Communication with teachers is of vital importance and can be done in a variety of ways: a pre-visit by a member of the project team to the school; an awareness-raising session for teachers of participating classes at the gallery; distribution of a preparatory information pack.
- be realistic in timetabling – allow time for pupils to get their coats off and on, time for juice breaks, time for clearing up.
- be flexible. There is always a difference in attitude and ability between children, even if they are of the same age.
- where possible, display the resulting work alongside the work which inspired it. An exhibition extends the workshop and gallery experience and is an official seal of approval of the value of the work produced.

DO NOT...

- give a lecture at the start. Children are always keen to get on with the practical work, therefore the introductory session should generally be brief and focused. Discussion should be encouraged as work progresses and question time should come at the end.
- allow adults to impose their own ideas onto the children. This should be made clear to teachers and adult helpers beforehand.

Hands On!
...object handling at Marischal Museum

The object handling session is probably the most widely advocated type of education provision in museums throughout Scotland, and beyond. All museums hold objects and, with due regard for the conservation needs of those objects, can provide controlled opportunities for handling them. Such opportunities further increase the power of the object to develop the skills of investigation and imaginative speculation important for life-long learning, and to enhance understanding in learners of all ages.

Marischal Museum, located within Marischal College, University of Aberdeen, has over the past few years developed a series of object handling workshops in collaboration with educators. These are related to popular school topics, and use material from many different areas of the museum's collections. An information pack for teachers contains general booking information and individual leaflets on each workshop, while the publication *Learning With Objects*, written for the museum by Kim Davidson on secondment from Slains Primary School, describes a variety of pre-visit activities which foster the skills necessary for learning with objects.

The format of the object handling workshops involves four sequenced activities:

- An initial discussion covers the children's experiences of museums, and introduces the idea of care and conservation of objects. The whole class is then involved in the investigation of four objects which are contextualised where possible through story-telling. At this stage the pupils are guided by the curator, so that they become familiar with the strategy for investigating objects: questioning, using multi-sensory exploration; describing; discussing; speculating; and coming to conclusions.

- The class is divided into four groups, each group being given a single object to investigate together. This encourages discussion among the group members and reinforces the questioning techniques used in the introductory stage, giving the pupils confidence when they come to investigate objects individually.

- After the addition of a number of other objects, each pupil is given an object recording sheet which encourages investigation and visual recording of one object in detail. Different versions of the sheet are used for classes studying different topics.

- Having put away the papers, boards and pencils, each group moves to another table. After a few minutes general scrutiny, one object is chosen from each table for the group to investigate. Ultimately a volunteer from each table is asked to talk about that object to the rest of the class.

As part of the Museums Education Initiative, Marischal Museum conducted an evaluation study using their approach to object handling to identify and describe the factors which best facilitate pupils learning from artefacts. The research findings have been published in the form of a report, *Hands on! Children's learning from objects in Marischal Museum* (Goolnik 1995), containing a preamble outlining the background and objectives of the study, a description of the methodology, and the conclusions of the researcher. The findings confirmed the value of object handling sessions as a core educational activity in museums, but revealed a number of implications for teachers and museum staff if object handling is to be fully effective. The format of Marischal

Museum's approach is fully explored, and can be used as a model for other museums, taking into consideration the implications, as detailed in the report. The report also highlighted the need for further research:

> *"This research report provides a beginning to what deserves to be further substantial research on a range of issues, and on a variety of approaches to include objects that pupils cannot be allowed to handle. Language development questions, different teaching and learning strategies, the problem of the provision of contextual knowledge relevant to objects being studied, the use of knowledge structures of different types in which to embed object study, are but some of the issues deserving further study. Curricular guidelines point up the value of museum work, further stressing the need for research in this area."*

SYDNEY WOOD, SOCIAL STUDIES
DEPT RESEARCH UNIT
NORTHERN COLLEGE OF
EDUCATION, ABERDEEN

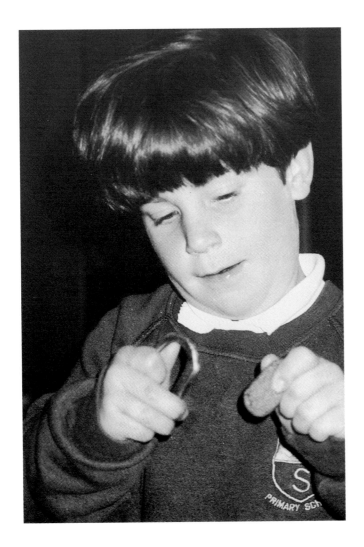

Trying to make a spark – using the flint and fleerie at Marischal Museum.

SUMMARY POINTS:

DO...

- allow pupils to handle high-quality, authentic objects that would not otherwise be possible.
- communicate with teachers to ensure that handling sessions are related to classroom study.
- make connections to the displays if the object handling takes place in the museum.
- use objects which have a dramatic impact during the class introductory session. The fun aspect of making something happen is highly motivational, capturing the interest of the children and making them more attentive.
- encourage discussion and speculation about past use by others.
- try to provide some contextual information to aid speculation about what it was used for and who might have used it. Only then is object handling effective in increasing pupils' understanding of the people connected with the objects.
- empower teachers to teach pupils the skills required to investigate objects beforehand.

There are a number of publications which assist teachers in developing the skills required for object investigation, but teachers like pupils learn most effectively if actively involved. Object handling sessions for teachers are an ideal way to reinforce the benefits as regards skills development, and to emphasise the necessity of careful handling. They can also be used to link in with the need for contextual knowledge.

DO NOT...

- use replicas unless there is no alternative and pupils know they are replicas.
- limit visual recording of an object to drawing. Children generally enjoy recording an object they have handled and investigated at first-hand. However, not all children are confident illustrators and alternative methods of visually recording objects should also be considered, such as photographing the object from different angles to get a complete record.

Theatre in Museum Education
...at Kirkcaldy Museum and Art Gallery

The video produced by Fife Museums Forum, *A Class of Their Own. The museum as a learning resource*, illustrates a number of different types of museum education provision in Fife's museums including *All at Sea*, a Theatre in Education workshop designed to interpret collections related to the maritime history of Kirkcaldy District.

WHAT IS THEATRE IN EDUCATION?

Theatre in Education uses an interactive dramatic performance to bring to life a subject for educational purposes. It is used in museum education to provide a context in which to interpret and illustrate the links between a wide range of material from a variety of sources: three-dimensional objects, photographs, paintings, costume, documents and even memories. It promotes understanding of what life was like for the people connected with these sources.

HOW DOES IT WORK AT KIRKCALDY?

The formula we now use at Kirkcaldy has evolved over a period of three years, building on the experiences and learning from the mistakes of three different workshops we developed in close collaboration with Fife College Theatre Arts Department.

- *The Queer-like Smell: Kirkcaldy's Linoleum Industry.*
- *All at Sea: The Maritime History of Kirkcaldy District.*
- *At Home in World War II: Home Front Life in Kirkcaldy.*

In all cases the museum's collections and strengths were the starting point. We chose objects for inclusion in the drama which might best convey the message of the exhibition being interpreted, and selected objects suitable for handling using the same criteria.

Storylines were developed jointly between the theatre group and the museum. For additional material for the script and character development we built up a general picture of the period through researching text books, local newspapers of the time, and from carrying out reminiscence sessions. If there were gaps in our knowledge requests were made through the local press for people to come forward with information. In all cases the subjects chosen drew upon a wealth of living memory which gave the performances an aura of credibility.

The workshops have been carried out most successfully in the museum itself, but we have also taken the performance, and the source material, out to schools and other venues.

The workshops are structured in four stages:

- Introduction (approximately 10 minutes)
  Ideally a member of the museum staff will establish relevance of the performance to the museum, and set the scene by taking the children back to the period in which the performance is set using mechanisms such as closing their eyes and imagining as period music or taped reminiscence is played. As part of this each child is given a very basic piece of costume to encourage participation in the performance.

● Scripted Performance (approximately 40 minutes)
  The children are seated for this. The aim is to get across the bulk of the information as the characters interact with each other and use the museum objects. The children are asked questions, drawn into the conversation, given tasks to perform. Some improvisation is necessary by the cast in order to encourage participation of the audience. The performance can move from one gallery space to another, working around the exhibits as the story unfolds.

● Activities (approximately 30 minutes)
  At this point the children are split into groups. Each cast member, still in character, works with a group which is then rotated. The smaller the group the better this works as the cast are able to draw out each individual child. The activities relate to the storyline and aim to help the children to understand the material better, or to introduce new information. They might involve: learning a skill, such as net making in *All at Sea*; handling and investigating original artefacts; trying on costume; or recapping on information they have already been introduced to as they help a cast member write a letter to a friend. The cast need to be well-informed about the period and the objects to be able to cope with awkward questions from the children.

● Conclusion (approximately 10 minutes)
  The children are brought back together and the performance concluded as the class are brought back to the present day.

The structure is designed to be extremely flexible. The scripted performance remains the same but the length and content of the activities can be adapted to suit the age group, size of audience, space available etc.

Although our Theatre in Education productions were originally developed for primary schools, we have in fact used them with a variety of audiences: mixed age groups, eg families; adults; special needs; secondary schools. Possibly the two most prohibitive factors involved in a project like this are the cost and the time involved in terms of research, assembling props and costumes, rehearsals, publicity, supervision of performances and maintenance. It is important, therefore, to get it 'right' during the preparation stages and to get as much mileage as possible out of all the hard work!

Susanna Hastilow
August 1995
Susanna Hastilow is Outreach Officer at Kirkcaldy Museum and Art Gallery

SUMMARY POINTS:

- Theatre in Education is an exciting way of interpreting museum collections. It provides a memorable and enjoyable experience for the audience, and excellent publicity for the museum.

- For schools it can provide a context for learning and contribute to a cross-curricular study in class, developing knowledge and understanding, a variety of skills, imagination, and informed attitudes about the world we live in.

- Possible costs include: commissioning script; fees for actors; expenses and travel for actors; costumes; additional props; teachers' packs.

- Collaboration with a local college theatre arts department is a low-cost way of accessing actors, scriptwriters and technical support for the museum. It is mutually beneficial, giving experience to students in all these areas.

- This is not just theatre in a museum space, but theatre about museum collections, therefore it is necessary to base scripts around what the museum has.

- Museums should work closely with the scriptwriter in order to achieve a balance between artistic concerns about creating 'good theatre', historical accuracy and relevance to the museum.

- Thorough research of the subject by museum staff and individual members of the cast is essential for scriptwriting, character development and acquiring background information for activities.

- Theatre works well in and around an exhibition space, using the exhibits as a backdrop. Other artefacts not normally on display can be brought in for the performance, thus widening access to collections.

- It is important to inform actors of the conservation needs of the objects they will be using so that they can encourage respect of the objects by the children during the activity sessions.

- Drawing up contracts for the actors, even if they are performing for a nominal fee or expenses only, encourages a professional approach.

- As with other forms of museum education provision, relevance to classroom study is essential. This can be achieved through: doing your homework to find out if the proposed production will fit in with topics being studied; circulating a first draft of the script for comment to teachers; producing a teachers' information pack; asking for details of what the class has covered already, plus any special needs, on the booking form in order to tailor the workshop more closely to the needs of the class.

- A teachers' information pack can provide general background information to the performance, and reproduce documents, photographs, images of the objects and transcripts of reminiscences around which the story was woven.

Pupils join the family for tea on the Home Front in World War II.

Designing *The Chinese Way*
...the importance of educational input into exhibition design

Traditionally, museum education services have provided school programmes, guided tours, outreach programmes, interpretive kits and publications aimed at helping different age-groups and kinds of visitors to make sense of exhibitions. Education staff were seldom concerned with planning exhibitions that, later, they were expected to interpret to the public. More recently however, museums have begun to recognise the important role for education staff in the design of exhibitions.

There are a number of reasons for this trend. First, there has been an increasing interest in museums in the role of exhibitions in communicating their message to a wider audience and the recognition of the diversity of this audience, needs and expectations. Second, the changes in the school curriculum throughout the United Kingdom has created a demand for museums to increase access to their displays by a younger audience.

Educators have experience in designing learning experiences. That process involves both research of the subject matter being taught and knowledge of how the audience is likely to respond. They have experience of planning for real people and they can visualise those who would have difficulty with any given experience. Lesson planning is relevant and useful experience in exhibition planning.

In response to the Scottish Museums Council's Museums Education Initiative, Glasgow Museums were invited to produce an exhibition that would use ethnographical materials in support of the Scottish schools curriculum. Glasgow Museums has an extensive ethnography collection and there were therefore various possible themes for the exhibition. The Chinese collection was chosen because of its range and quality and its appropriateness to the curriculum. It was decided to target the learning outcomes of the Environmental Studies curriculum which dealt with People and the Past, People and Place, and People and Society for Level D which should be attainable for pupils aged between 10 and 12 years.

The exhibition aims were clearly defined:

- to create opportunities for pupils to gain an understanding of the origins of certain aspects of Chinese life through investigation;
- to help pupils understand the value for Chinese people in maintaining their customs and traditions while living in this country;
- to make the museum visit stimulating, enjoyable and purposeful for pupils; and
- to offer a unique learning experience that could not be provided by other resources.

The aims of the project had specific implications for exhibition content and interpretation, and for material provided for use by teachers and pupils. We wanted to create an exhibition that would encourage active on-site learning in a museum context. Within Glasgow Museums this was the first time an exhibition had been put on specifically for the school curriculum. A multi-professional team was formed to devise the exhibition, consisting of curatorial, conservation and design staff and led by a member of the education staff.

The specialist knowledge of the curator was essential in teasing out the themes of the exhibition by relating the availability of the objects within the collection to the needs of the curriculum. A major difficulty after this stage was to create a balance between the display style favoured by the education staff and the restrictions imposed by the needs of conservation. The core collection could not provide objects for handling and certain objects could not be put on open display except by purchasing special equipment which was beyond the resources of the project. This

Interactive displays in *The Chinese Way*.

meant that some artefacts had to be purchased, and replicas made of others. The designer took a proactive role in reconciling the need to display the objects safely but sympathetically, and to incorporate particular learning activities within displays. Throughout the process the education staff insisted that the criteria for solving any problems in connection with the selection of objects, the method of display or level of text and interaction was determined by the needs of the target audience, in this case schoolchildren.

Being led by educational aims meant an approach to exhibition content which curatorial and conservation colleagues found difficult. The exhibition did not try to create an accessible summary of a branch of an academic subject, nor did it seek to show the 'best' objects from the Chinese collection; in fact many of these were left out. It used the objects only when they helped achieve the aims of the exhibition. While members of the public and school parties may not have had access to a comprehensive show about China, and may not have seen all the best objects in the collection, they had far greater access to the learning potential of the objects than would have been the case in a traditionally conceived exhibition.

The resulting exhibition was displayed in St Mungo's Museum of Religious Life and Art for five months (including two months of school holidays) and was visited by over 6,000 schoolchildren.

Evaluation of the schools' response was made through a questionnaire. In general, almost all visiting teachers were pleased with the various aspects of *The Chinese Way* and considered it an appropriate model for future exhibitions:

"We enjoyed our visit and would recommend that you try something like this again."

"I look forward to many more of these 'hands-on' introductions to other topics."

"I would welcome more of this type of exhibition on other cultures."

Pupils responses echoed these same points:

"I think it was all very good and I am sure many other people will like it as much as I did."

Though there were no direct monitoring of the general visitor of whom 100,000 visited St Mungo's during the run of the exhibition, there is some indication that there was a favourable response to the exhibition. Museum assistants reported informally that visitors had praised the hands-on approach; this was reflected in some of the comment left on the board in the museum:

"Let's have more of this type of exhibition."

"We had a lot of fun with this exhibition."

The comments from museum assistants who staffed the exhibition were generally enthusiastic. Although interactive and open display demand more supervision from museum staff, this was seen as a positive rather than a negative factor. Staff welcomed the opportunity of becoming more involved with visitors and interacting with them. They also felt in many ways the provision of interactives made supervision easier, since they provide children, whether in formal or informal groups, with activities which involve their interest.

The Chinese Way provides an appropriate model for future exhibitions in Glasgow Museums in so far as it demonstrates that a multi-disciplinary team drawn from curatorial, design and educational staff can co-operate effectively and creatively to address the needs of the school curriculum. Nevertheless, there are wider and more general implications which can be drawn from the successful methodology adopted for this exhibition.

First, exhibit planning, design and installation had to start by identifying the message, or messages and work backwards to the objects, layout, presentation media and formats most likely to convey the message.

Interactive display in *The Chinese Way.*

There is a vast amount of information available about the intended audience, in this case school children aged 10–12. This directly affected exhibition content and presentation. Such information included data on the knowledge, attitudes and expectations of the children and their teachers. The most important educational goals of the exhibition – primary messages, what visitors are expected to do, feel and learn – were able to be carefully identified and combined with this information.

A great deal of attention was given to ways to motivate visitors involvement with the content of key exhibits. The emphasis was to be on providing active learning opportunities, and allowing each individual child to proceed at his or her own pace. A fun element was included in each part of the design stage. There was a recognition that lots of activity at popular exhibits does not necessarily mean that useful ideas are being conveyed. Rewarding features were built in the design to encourage visitors to give focused attention to exhibit content, visuals and text. For example, visitors were asked to make comparisons, discover answers to leading questions, try on costume, complete a story or solve a problem. Most visitors notice objects, pictures, movement and action elements more than they do text. Interest generated by the activity encouraged visitors to seek more information from text, graphics or other materials. The text was easily and quickly found, as close to the object as possible, well illuminated, using large print and having high contrast.

Objects, illustrations, text, headings, questions and processes used familiar, active language and visual formats whenever possible.

Visitor flow was a crucial element in this exhibition. The layout allowed small groups to be actively absorbed around the exhibition themes for a reasonable time. Flitting or moving quickly from one exhibit to the next was thereby discouraged. This enabled easy management of the exhibition for class size groups and contributed to effective use by families at weekends.

Observations of the behaviour of visitors within the exhibition allowed certain minor adjustments to be made to the sign posting, headings, text and graphics after it opened.

Thus the key elements in the preparation of a lesson can be seen to have direct implications for exhibition design. They are:

- know your audience;
- decide what message or messages you want to get over;
- decide on your strategy for teaching and learning at each stage, eg discussion, experiment, investigation, observation;
- select these resources (objects, audio visual photographs, etc);
- remember fun is a powerful motivator and learning tool.

The potential of museums as places for alternative educational enrichment will require some time before it can be fully realised. Good communication should be based on a sound understanding of the visitor and how they learn. Maintaining a clear focus on this approach can create an opportunity for museums to maximise on the skills of all their professional staff, especially the educator in communicating their message.

Jem Fraser
18 July 1995
Jem Fraser is Principal Education Officer for Strathclyde Museums Education Service and is based at the Kelvingrove Museum and Art Gallery, Glasgow. Maureen Finn, who led this project, is now Education Officer at Camden Arts Centre, London.

5–14 at the Grampian Transport Museum ... the production of a teachers' information pack

Information packs are one of the most commonly used methods of informing teachers about the museum and its resources, and helping them to prepare for visits. Aimed at teachers rather than at pupils, they are a flexible means of conveying a wealth of information and advice which teachers can sift through and adapt to suit their own classroom study and the different levels of ability of their own pupils.

The project at the Grampian Transport Museum grew out of the curator's desire to improve the quality of the learning experience at the museum for school groups. The museum concentrates on the road and rail transport history of the North East of Scotland, with the greater emphasis placed on road travel, and has been well established as a destination for school visits, proving popular with both staff and pupils. It was felt, however, that although the 'fun' element was firmly in place, a more significant educational benefit should be aspired to.

Grampian Region Education Department assigned a Curriculum Development Officer to the project to assist the staff in identifying themed study areas where the formation of hands-on investigative activities would involve pupils actively working with large scale objects, vehicles, tools, and archive materials only available at the museum.

The Curriculum Development Officer used her knowledge of the curriculum to link the activities within each theme to a grid displaying all the components, attainment outcomes and key features of Environmental Studies 5–14, making additional links to Maths 5–14 where appropriate. The themes were audited on this grid with highlighted areas showing all the links it would be possible for teachers to cover. Teachers were encouraged to use the grids as a working document. Blank spaces were left for notes, forward planning and to record ideas for follow-up activities.

A teachers' information pack was seen to be the ideal way to:

- inform teachers of the developments at the Grampian Transport Museum and market the new approach;
- encourage integration of a visit to the museum into a planned programme of classroom study through providing suggestions for preparatory and follow-up work, historical and technological information about the exhibits, suggestions for activities on site, and links to the curriculum; and
- encourage independent use of the exhibits by teachers and pupils in the absence of museum staff with suggestions of how to manage the visit.

The proposed activities and the information pack were piloted with a local school at an early stage. This was time-consuming to organise and run, but the benefits were far reaching. It was an excellent way of extending partnership links with the local schools, and the museum had the opportunity to correct any flaws in the activities or resource materials before they were produced in final format.

The pack was produced in loose leaf format within a glossy folder. Considering the quality of the pack, it was relatively inexpensive to produce. Museum staff did almost all of the work for the pack themselves. Once all the text had been written, and images chosen, they put together a layout using photocopied pictures and copy from a wordprocessor, presenting the printer with a complete pack. The printer simply screened and scanned all the images and changed the typeface. If museums have access to desk top publishing facilities, very high quality packs can be produced in-house.

The pack was given a high profile launch and distributed to all schools in Grampian using the Education Department's internal mailing system. If an information pack is to be of benefit to teachers and museum staff, it is imperative that teachers are aware of why it is being produced and how to use it. At the Grampian Transport Museum, the pack was envisaged as being a tool for a teacher-led visit to ease the pressure on museum staff, but many schools still arrived without adequate preparation and had to be carried through the visit. It would seem that the value of a pre-visit which allows teachers to familiarise themselves with the displays, try out the activities, and speak to museum staff needed more emphasis in the pack. If a pre-visit is unrealistic because of distance, then a telephone call to discuss the class visit is an alternative method of supplementing the information in the pack.

CHECKLIST FOR PRODUCING A TEACHER'S INFORMATION PACK
General information which can be inserted into any future resource pack can include:

- an introduction to the museum and the services it provides for schools
- a location map, plus how to get there/where to park information
- advice on planning a visit, including opportunities for pre-visit
- booking information
- orientation: what to do on arrival; facilities for lunches; disabled access; plan of exhibition area, indicating toilets
- advice on managing a school visit.

More specific information is needed to help teachers prepare their pupils and to integrate the visit into classroom study. This can include:

- how to use the pack
- background information on themes
- links to the curriculum
- suggestions for preparatory activities before the visit
- information about key exhibits – contextual and technological
- suggestions for activities to do at the museum
- suggestions for follow-up activities to do back in the classroom
- information about specific museum staff-led activities available at the museum
- a glossary of unfamiliar terminology
- availability of other resources to support the themes
- evaluation sheet.

Packs of one form or another were produced to encourage good practice in the use of a variety of different types of provision during the Museums Education Initiative, among which were: the interactive exhibition created by *Operation Move It!*; the exhibition, resource and object loan packs devised for *People at Work*; the workstations and interpretive workshops involved in *In*

Touch With The Past; the temporary exhibition, *The Chinese Way*; and the touring exhibition and outreach ceramic workshops developed in *Earth Art*. Some of these packs included reproduced source material: extracts from documents or newspapers; photographs, effectively becoming resource as well as information packs.

Others have included pupil worksheets which a majority of teachers seem to expect museums to produce in spite of the fact that a worksheet designed for general use risks failing both to address the issue of differentiation within a group and the tasks and skills they have come to develop. That is not to say there is no place for worksheets in museums, they can in fact provide an effective focus for a visit if they result from joint effort, with museums providing basic suggestions which teachers can tailor to the particular needs of their own pupils.

CHECKLIST FOR CONSTRUCTING A MUSEUM WORKSHEET

DO...

- rename it. The term activity sheets sounds much more inviting and more accurately describes what goes on in a museum.
- decide what it is you want the pupils to learn, and construct activities which will bring that learning about.
- design activities which involve pupils in working in groups to encourage discussion and speculation.
- avoid congestion around exhibits by giving each group different learning outcomes, involving investigation of different objects.
- design activities which direct observation on to the object.
- encourage pupils to make links to other objects, by asking for comparisons, similarities, differences.
- ask for descriptions and opinions rather than right or wrong answers.
- ask for some kind of visual recording, whether it be detailed drawing, sketching or taking photographs.
- make sure the information gathered is followed up back in the classroom.

DO NOT...

- make the activity sheet too long and complicated, so that the children spend all their time at the museum filling in the sheet, rather than enjoying the experience.
- design activities which involve pupils in label copying.
- ask questions to which there is only one 'right' answer.
- ask questions which only require the answer 'yes' or 'no'.
- ask questions which can be answered without necessarily coming to the museum at all.

The Craigievar Express is still in good working order at the Grampian Transport Museum.

Artefacts on Loan

A popular method of giving schools access to museum collections has been through the provision of a loans service of themed object handling boxes which relate to the curriculum. Such services range from the small-scale, which depends on teachers fetching and carrying back the boxes themselves, to the extensive service with a large menu of themes, which demands complex organisation in the administration, delivery and collection of boxes.

There are a number of advantages to providing a loans service:

- it raises the profile of the museum with local schools;
- it allows for independent use of the collections by teachers to prepare for and follow up a museum visit;
- it allows teachers to further develop skills required for investigating museum objects;
- once developed, a loans box is a long-term resource;
- as a one-off project, the production of a loans box may attract local sponsorship; and
- for museums without education officers, the production of a loans box provides an attractive placement opportunity for a local teacher.

Problems associated with this type of provision are in the main related to the administration and maintenance of the service which can be costly, time-consuming and soul-destroying if artefacts are damaged or lost. Whether a service is large or small it requires well organised booking procedures and careful monitoring of returns with regard to the packing and care of the artefacts.

Two of the Museums Education Initiative projects involved the production of loans boxes, each for different reasons.

FALKIRK MUSEUMS

As part of the project, *People at Work*, Falkirk Museums produced three loans boxes of authentic, robust objects, taken from the collections held at Grangemouth Museum Workshop and Stores, which is currently open to schools for only three weeks of the year. The Workshop acts as the main store for the collections of the Museum Service, which represent the working life of the Forth valley. *People at Work* looks at the development of agriculture, crafts and trades, and heavy industry in the area around Falkirk and Grangemouth. It aims to encourage a positive attitude to the local environment through investigating the industrial heritage of the area.

Butter making equipment at Grangemouth Museum Workshop and Stores.

The object handling boxes are available with teachers' notes, and provide a taster of tools, equipment and products displayed at the Workshop itself. They can also be used to give access to the collections when the Workshop is closed, fulfilling one of the main aims of the Museum Service which was to overcome the problem of limited access for school groups to the Workshop, and to find ways of making this important, yet underused collection more accessible through the development of outreach opportunities.

GROAM HOUSE MUSEUM

At Groam House Museum, which is presented and promoted as a Pictish Interpretive Centre for Ross and Cromarty, two Pictish loans boxes were developed to underpin features within Environmental Studies 5–14 and to provide opportunities for interpretation through Expressive Arts 5–14.

The main collection at the museum consists of one large cross slab together with 14 fragments of carved Pictish stones, display panels, and hangings. The strength of the museum and its Pictish stones lies in the fact that they all originated in Rosemarkie and that they date back to the 8th century AD when Rosemarkie was an extremely important early Christian site.

Since the changes in the school curriculum it was noticed that more schools were visiting the museum, especially when covering in class the Celts/Vikings and more recently the Picts specifically. School parties are always welcome, but, because of the compact nature and layout of the museum, a number of educational activities such as role play cannot be undertaken on site. The curator decided that the best way forward was to take the 'museum' to the schools, and to provide a set of loans boxes, filled with suitable replica material, such as costumes, leather goods, jewellery, casts of the stones for rubbing, a weaving frame and a reproduction harp. The intention was to give pupils an educational 'taste' of the Picts, thus putting a follow-up visit to see and discuss the genuine stones into context.

Although not normally encouraged, the use of replicas in this instance was entirely appropriate in that it is a physical impossibility to take the real evidence out of the museum and into the classroom. Investigation of the replica objects allows pupils to gain an insight into what kind of people the Picts were, and wets the appetite for a visit to see something that was truly made by these people.

Putting together a loans box was a new experience for Groam House Museum. At Dundee Museum there is a long history of providing a school loan service.

DUNDEE MUSEUM

Dundee Museum has offered an extensive loan service to schools for 20 years. The kits are made up of three-dimensional objects and specimens from the Natural and Human History collections, models, photographs, posters, maps, and information and suggestions. They cover a wide range of topics – from Early Man, Picts, and Romans to Victorians and World War II as well as birds, mammals, shells, minibeasts, fossils and trees. Most of the models, specially commissioned, relate to Dundee – a Tay Ferry, a local tramcar, or a 19th-century dock scene. Posters have been designed to feature local customs, industries, celebrities and parks. All are useful in assisting with local studies.

Most of the loan kits have been produced by listening to and working with teachers, and by responding to various curricula initiatives, as well as reflecting the museum displays.
A recent request came from a group of secondary science teachers who wanted material to help illustrate their introductory course for all S1 pupils. The course concentrated on the Classification of Living Things as well as their Diversity of Structural Form. In the past they had borrowed a few specimens but had never liked to ask for more than the three kits we suggested as a maximum in our catalogue.

After several discussions with the teachers who drew up a 'wish list' and a timetable for borrowing, the Education Officer liaised with a member of the Natural History staff. Discussions took place and by the beginning of the school session a 'mini display' of specimens and a timetable for borrowing to suit individual workplans had been produced. Notes and extra information were also supplied. The schools devised their own activity booklets to be used with the loan material. The kit is being assessed by the schools and suggestions for change are being fed into the museum.

Responding to changing needs and new initiatives ensures continuing use of the loan service which in turn encourages groups to visit the museum.

Nancy Davey
September 1995
Nancy Davey is Education Officer at Dundee Museum

SUMMARY POINTS FOR THE PRODUCTION AND USE OF A LOAN BOX:

DO...

- support thematic teaching and learning in schools, and choose themes in collaboration with educators.
- allow time for preparation including: researching themes; identifying and selecting the objects and other source material; designing the packaging; and writing accompanying teachers' notes.
- include high quality original artefacts whenever possible. These can be obtained as duplicate material from the main collection, or as material specifically collected or purchased for educational use and not accessioned into the main collection.
- complement three-dimensional objects with photographs, printed archives and documents to show how different sources link up to give us a fuller picture.
- choose boxes which are light, strong and easily carried. Packaging should hold the objects securely inside.
- empower teachers to use the boxes effectively. The value of the loan box in classroom depends on the understanding and the skills of teachers in the use of objects. Explicit teachers' notes can help, but interactive awareness-raising sessions are more effective. Some museum services make it a prerequisite that teachers attend a session themselves before they can take out a loan box for their pupils. At such a session the 'value' of the object is discussed and teachers are taught how to handle objects sensitively.
- establish clear booking and collection procedures at the outset.
- display a list of contents on the inside of the lid. An identical ticklist should be included in the box which the teacher should complete and sign on return of the box, noting any damaged or missing items.
- ask teachers to write short notes on how they used the box. This doubles as evaluation for the museum and as a handbook of case studies which can be helpful for other teachers.

DO NOT...

- use replicas unless there is a valid reason for doing so and pupils are made aware that they are replicas.
- encourage use of loan boxes as a substitute for a museum visit. In rural areas loan boxes will sometimes be the only way pupils can get access to a museum's collections, but where possible it should provide preparatory activities to whet the appetite, or follow-up activities to consolidate a visit.

Heard but not seen... a new approach to outreach at the National Galleries of Scotland

Any attempt to define a series of principles which would cover all the possible meanings of the words 'Museum Education' may be doomed to failure within a couple of sentences. Still, it is worth a try. Education in museums and galleries can involve imparting facts, figures and information and it can also involve suggesting a variety of ways of looking and thinking which may be quite different from the ways we usually look and think. But much more important than any of the above, in my opinion, is the potential all gallery and museum collections have for exciting the capacity for wonder. There is a kind of interest, and therefore a kind of delight, to be found in the least and most apparently uninspiring object or work of art in any gallery or museum collection. Our job as museum educators should be to convey a sense of that interest and demonstrate the possibility of that delight. The important thing we should all remember (something which all of us occasionally forget) is that these responses need to be generated by dealing with real things: original paintings, sculpture, prints, drawings, photographs, real shards of Roman pottery, real pieces of Jacobite memorabilia, real steam engines, etc, not reproductions.

So when we in the Education Department of the National Galleries of Scotland started thinking about outreach materials, teachers' packs, distance learning tools, we wanted to reproduce something which would stimulate interest in real works of art but which did so without placing too much emphasis on the use of reproductions, or if reproductions were involved we wanted everyone to be clear that that was what they were. I always worry when children are unimpressed at their first glimpse of a real Monet because they have 'done' the Impressionists at school from books, slides, posters, etc.

That led us to experimenting with the audio-tapes we have tentatively entitled *Heard but not seen* – taped conversations with children from Edinburgh in which they/we describe, discuss, explore verbally a number of works from the Galleries' collections. The tapes are edited down to about 10 minutes in length and they include physical descriptions, imaginative allusions, references to images with which the children are familiar and very importantly, they preserve a sense of the excitement felt by the speakers as the conversation and the process of exploration progress.

They are then sent, without any visuals, to classes of children who have never seen the works themselves. These children listen to the tapes, making verbal or pictorial notes from which they can make drawings, paintings, sculpture of their own, re-inventing the originals in the process. We are finding that this 'reproduction in sound' can actually provide the listening children with more useful (and certainly more imaginative and enticing) information about a work of art than a pictorial reproduction would. And it has an extra added advantage: there is no way in which it can be confused with the real thing.

After all this work has been done, when the desire to see what the originals look like is almost unbearable, the class can either arrange to visit the gallery or be sent a traditional reproduction (– which is, of course, quite different from the real thing at least we now all know that). At the end of the process the children are not necessarily any closer to seeing a real work of art than they were at the beginning but at least by then they all want to; maybe they will be able to visit the galleries in Edinburgh at some point in their school career or afterwards (there is life after school . . .) And even if that does not happen, maybe they will attempt to see original works of whatever kind wherever they can find them: paintings in the local stately home, the sculpture on the war memorial in the village square, etc. There are more 'real things' around than you might think.

It is just possible, of course, that the children might simply become frustrated and irritated at their inability to get to a gallery. So far, at least, that has not happened. But if it does maybe a little irritant applied at the right moment might be no bad thing.

Michael Cassin
August 1995
Michael Cassin is Head of Education at the National Galleries of Scotland

Part 4
TRAINING: The Basics

Training plays a major part in developing any area of expertise and museum education is no exception. Training in museum education can be developed at many different levels to meet the needs of both the teaching profession and a whole variety of museum workers: managers, administrators, curators, conservators, documentation officers, designers, attendants, museum assistants, technicians and volunteers.

TRAINING IN MUSEUM EDUCATION FOR TEACHERS

There is as yet no systematic approach throughout Scotland to developing museum education as a prescribed element of teacher education in either pre-service or in-service training, despite acknowledgment of the value of resources beyond the classroom to support the curriculum.

In colleges of education any pre-service training in the use of museum collections is often only instated on an informal basis through the enthusiasm, and belief in its worth, of individual lecturers who have developed good relationships with local museums. Similarly in-service training events for teachers are generally locally stimulated initiatives, dependent either on the enthusiasm of individual museums/schools, or on the fact that the museum has in place, as museum education officer, a teacher seconded from the education authority itself.

The National Curriculum in England and Wales, with its express requirement that teachers use resources outwith the classroom to support the work going on in the classroom, led to a significant increase in demand for access to museum collections by school groups which was seldom matched by an equivalent increase in museum staff time to service this demand. A solution to the problem has manifested itself in the current trend in museums towards providing support for teachers by way of in-service training and information packs, empowering them to use the displays independently with their pupils, to focus on the outcomes, and to tailor the visit to their own requirements. Thus a single two-hour in-service course, attended by 15 teachers, can reach up to 450 pupils, and ultimately even more as teachers use the knowledge and skills acquired with new classes in subsequent years. This trend is now growing in Scotland, where the large numbers of museums without education officers are finding it more appropriate to their role as facilitators rather than deliverers of educational programmes, and are benefiting through direct communication with teachers at in-service courses.

INSET, PAT SESSIONS AND TWILIGHT SESSIONS

Training for teachers can range from initial awareness-raising sessions which do little more than illustrate the potential of learning through museum collections to support the curriculum, to those carried out for a specific purpose, such as to encourage sensitive and effective use of a loan service. Furthermore, training can be offered formally as part of the Local Education Authority's staff development programme of In-service Training (INSET) courses, or informally during Planned Activity Time (PAT) and 'twilight' sessions which are held after school finishes for the day.

Planned Activity Time (PAT) is the period of time, approximately one hour per week, that every primary and secondary school in Scotland is now required to lay aside for staff development. When this is taken varies from region to region. In some regions all schools are timetabled to hold PAT sessions on the same day, at the same time every week. Other regions have allowed schools their own choice of day and time. PAT sessions provide museums and teachers with an ideal opportunity to get together without the restrictions of the more formal programme of INSET courses organised by the Local Education Authority which are generally held during teaching time and require headteachers to find and pay for supply cover for the teacher attending the course. During a PAT session, which can be held at the museum or at the school, museum staff can: inform teachers about educational provision/special events at the museum; brief teachers on how to use loan boxes; hold a handling session to help teachers develop skills in object analysis which they can then pass on to their pupils; provide access to the expertise of the curator for contextual information with regard to specific exhibitions/displays; listen to teachers' requirements for the coming session; and work together with teachers to determine future developments and possible piloting of activities/resource materials. The possibilities are numerous.

Headteachers along with management teams and staff decide on curriculum priorities for in-service training for the session. These usually emanate from the school's development plan. Headteachers then identify staff development needs within those priorities. Museums can therefore contact headteachers to discuss ways in which museum education can provide staff development opportunities which target those areas of need. Similarly headteachers can take the initiative and contact their local museum if training in the use of resources beyond the classroom is on the agenda.

Each of the pilot projects supported by the Museums Education Initiative offered an element of in-service training for teachers, either formally or informally. Those museums whose education officers are teachers seconded from the Local Education Authority, such as Strathclyde Museums Education Service and Falkirk Museums, were able to take advantage of that connection in order to articulate with the Authority's programme of INSET courses. Similarly the Education Officer at the Western Isles, which is already a unitary authority, had no difficulty in accessing INSET. 'Twilight' and PAT sessions were used by other museum services who had not been aware far enough in advance of the opportunities presented by INSET, the annual schedule for which is generally drawn up at the beginning of the school session. 'Twilight' and PAT sessions offered greater flexibility and museums were either able to target specific schools or encourage more widespread attendance using the internal mailing system of the Authority.

Case Study:

TEACHING TEACHERS – A STRATEGY FOR INSET AT FALKIRK MUSEUMS

'Be prepared' applies just as much to teachers and pupils visiting museums as guides on a camping expedition. The original in-service programme for training teachers in the Falkirk area was set up more than five years ago partially in response to ill-prepared classes visiting Falkirk Museums, but also in response to the many individual queries from teachers and invitations from headteachers to give talks to teachers.

Margaret Bowden helps teachers to investigate raw materials used by *People at Work*.

As there is only one member of full-time staff dedicated to education it was difficult to satisfy everyone's needs. Rather than reacting to demand, we set up a programme, in consultation with Central Region Education Department, whereby nowadays specific groups and geographical areas are targeted, and one or two members of staff from each school or department attend the training evenings. They are encouraged to report back to the rest of the staff, to share resources, and to prepare themselves, their pupils and their accompanying helpers for museum visits. Over the years there has been a noticeable improvement in how teachers approach visits. The more guidance and contextual information given to teachers, the more successful the visit and the more effective use made of the museums.

As Falkirk Museums Service is made up of several properties and sites of differing size, content, emphasis and educational potential, this is reflected in the type of INSET offered. A new course has been devised recently to help teachers make self-guided visits to the new exhibition, *People at Work*, developed as part of the Museums Education Initiative. A guided tour of the Museum Workshop and Stores in Grangemouth, guidance, useful hints and opportunities to study resources through handling sessions are built in to the course. Teachers can experience the educational activities which have been integrated into the displays and find out how the new exhibition dovetails with existing displays at Grangemouth Museum and resources on the Canals. At the end of each course teachers complete a form to indicate their level of satisfaction, and suggestions for the future. We take these into account when planning further courses. They are included with a yearly report sent to the Principal Officer of Falkirk Museums and the Director of Education.

The training courses are organised well in advance. As part of Central Region's Education Service, the museum education officer sends bids for staff development in January for the following academic year. The bids consist of information about proposed dates, target curricular areas, and content description, along with estimated cost including supply cover to release teachers from school, travelling expenses and the cost of tutors where appropriate. For the first time, the in-service programme has been included as part of the optional day courses rather than after school and consequently we are running practical workshops such as spinning and drama as well as the usual handling sessions. As many schools have devolved budgets, we will not know until June 1996 whether 'after school' versus 'day' courses are more popular. We carried out a survey two years ago which showed that teachers preferred to attend during the day when they were more alert, rather than after work, but early indications are that financial restrictions may be the deciding factor.

There are considerable advantages to be gained from a close working relationship with the local authority education department. These include administrative and financial help in organising the courses and help from advisers, while, as part of the official Staff Development Programme, the courses are given credibility and are more easily brought to the attention of members of staff by headteachers.

Margaret Bowden
Margaret Bowden is currently employed by Central Region Education Authority as Education Officer for Falkirk Museums Service

Case Study:

IN-SERVICE TRAINING AT THE NATIONAL MUSEUMS OF SCOTLAND (NMS)

The National Museums of Scotland has been concentrating in recent years on providing support aimed at teachers, with the aim of enabling as many teachers as possible to become more skilled in using a museum and its resources. This support takes two forms.

NMS has created a series of information packs for teachers which are firmly linked to the 5–14 Guidelines. These packs are intended to be used by the teacher before a visit and offer clear and detailed support for the planning of a visit. The packs are based around popular galleries or individual museums and help a teacher to focus on the key skills of collecting evidence, interpreting and evaluating evidence and recording and presenting evidence.

NMS also trains teachers directly through its Schools Officer. Different types of training are offered, ranging from very specific training related to using a particular set of objects or a particular gallery, to more general training looking at how a museum visit can develop various skills. Such training takes place both in the museum and in schools, through INSET or Planned Activity Time.

Since NMS has a national remit, it is felt important to provide resources for all Scottish schools. Accordingly the Schools Officer also travels to other regions to hold training sessions looking at the use of museums in general. The aim here is to encourage teachers to increase their use of museums as a resource, wherever they happen to be.

NMS feels that training of teachers as opposed to direct teaching of children is a more cost-effective way of reaching a wide audience and will in the long term enable more teachers to make better use of museums.

Ewan Small
Ewan Small is Schools Officer with the National Museums of Scotland

TRAINING IN MUSEUM EDUCATION FOR MUSEUM STAFF

In museums, an increase in the provision of training in museum education for those behind the scenes who collaborate to create displays for the visitor, as well as for those who deal directly with the visitor, stems from the realisation by management of the benefits education brings to the museum as a whole, raising its profile and giving the public greater physical and intellectual access to its collections. The incorporation of educational goals into a whole range of museum policies within the Forward Plan can provide the basis of a programme of in-service training for museum staff which addresses their needs in order that those educational goals might be attained. Thus education becomes an integral part of the museum service.

For those in direct contact with teachers and pupils, training in museum education can develop from training in customer care. Administrators responsible for telephone bookings are often the first point of contact for schools, therefore it is imperative that they have a sound knowledge about the services currently on offer so that they can give informed advice to teachers interested in bringing school groups to the museum or using a loans service. They can also be briefed to acquire the essential information the museum requires about a group coming to visit.

If the visit is to be teacher-led the role of attendants can be crucial in reinforcing the educational messages of the displays. Attendants often have extensive knowledge about the exhibits, and if they are aware of the context in which the displays are likely to be used by schools, they can provide information and direction where appropriate which will enhance the learning experience for pupils. In a number of museums and with certain types of exhibition which encourage multi-sensory investigation of exhibits, such as the 'Discovery Room' at the National Museums of Scotland, staff are employed on special temporary contracts and trained to deliver education programmes which have been created by educators working in collaboration with museum professionals. With this type of exhibition regular attendant staff can also have a part to play, but in order to do so may need to learn new skills in communication which further their own personal development. This need is recognised in the inclusion of the Unit, *Prepare and Deliver an Interpretive Event*, in the Level 3 Scottish/National Vocational Qualification in Collection Care and Visitor Services.

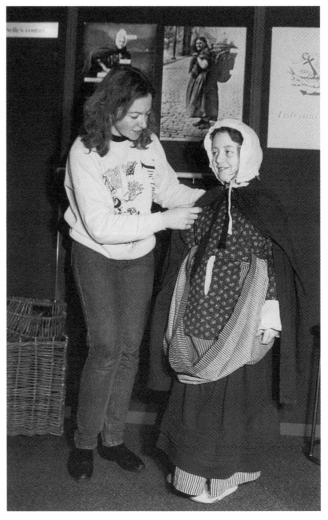

Facilitating in the Discovery Room at the National Museums of Scotland.

SCOTTISH/NATIONAL VOCATIONAL QUALIFICATIONS

The introduction of Scottish/National Vocational Qualifications (S/NVQs) offer a new dimension to training and development, and recognition for the individual working in the museums and galleries sector. The flexible nature of S/NVQs with their framework of *Units* which are broken down into *elements,* offer candidates the opportunity to progress at their own pace and achieve a qualification in the workplace through the assessment of their competence against nationally recognised standards.

At Levels 3–5 the qualifications comprise an agreed number of compulsory Units but also include a list of optional Units from which the candidate must select a specified number. This allows the candidate to work towards a qualification which is closely tied to their particular area of museum work. This system also enables individuals to progress through levels or acquire additional Units as their own career develops.

There is no qualification centred on education as such, but Units in the specialism of museum education are included in the overall framework. For example, the Level 4 S/NVQ in the Collection Management and Interpretation consists of six compulsory Units and four options. Candidates whose area of responsibility includes museum education could select as one option the Unit entitled F8 Plan and deliver interpretive activities. This Unit comprises five elements: F8.1 Plan the use of resources to deliver an interpretive activity; F8.2 Deliver an interpretive activity; F8.3 Provide an activity which supports learning objectives; F8.4 Provide opportunities for people to explore ideas; and F8.5 Develop information materials to support an interpretive activity. All five elements must be achieved for the Unit to be awarded. Further information on S/NVQs is available from the Museum Training Institute.

SCOTTISH MUSEUM COUNCIL'S TRAINING PROGRAMME:
MUSEUM BASICS – DEVELOPING A MUSEUM EDUCATION SERVICE

The training course, 'Museum Basics: Developing A Museum Education Service', was created, in partnership with the Council's training service, in response to the *Survey's* findings that, despite a minority of Scotland's museums having direct access to the expertise and knowledge of professional education staff, the vast majority were providing some sort of education service to schools. The training course focused on presenting to participants, mainly curators, the mechanisms by which in these circumstances they could facilitate the provision of an education service for schools which fully supported the curriculum.

A pre-course exercise had encouraged participants to assess the resources available to them in developing an education service for schools. During the practical sessions they were further encouraged to bear that assessment in mind, and relate the activities to their own collections and particular situation in order to determine what they might realistically be able to offer. At the end of the course each of the participants was asked to complete an action plan indicating points for immediate implementation which would lead to the fulfilment of long-term goals.

The sessions examined:

- the structure of the Scottish education system for pupils aged 5 to 18, in particular the 5–14 curriculum and the implications for museums;
- the strategy for learning through museum objects, and how it underpins the development of knowledge and understanding, skills and informed attitudes within the 5–14 curriculum;
- the thematic, cross-curricular approach to teaching and learning, highlighting popular topics and matching these to museum collections;
- the networks and mechanisms within the Scottish education system which can be used by museum staff to find out about the needs of the target audience and to obtain advice and assistance in product development, marketing and evaluation;
- the advantages and disadvantages of different types of educational provision.

Furthermore, the course promoted the benefits of assimilating an education policy into the museum's development plan, leading participants through the practical steps required to set one in place.

Strategy to set up and review an education policy

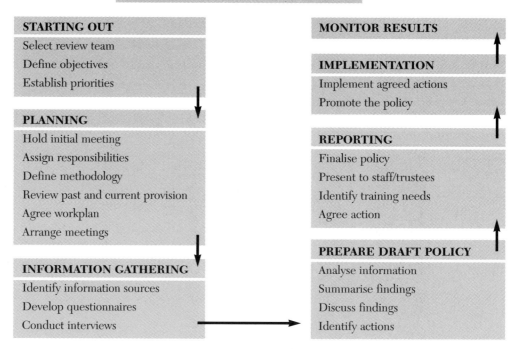

ISSUES TO ADDRESS
Resources available to the museum
Needs of target audience
Advantages/disadvantages of types of provision

STARTING OUT
Select review team
Define objectives
Establish priorities

PLANNING
Hold initial meeting
Assign responsibilities
Define methodology
Review past and current provision
Agree workplan
Arrange meetings

INFORMATION GATHERING
Identify information sources
Develop questionnaires
Conduct interviews

MONITOR RESULTS

IMPLEMENTATION
Implement agreed actions
Promote the policy

REPORTING
Finalise policy
Present to staff/trustees
Identify training needs
Agree action

PREPARE DRAFT POLICY
Analyse information
Summarise findings
Discuss findings
Identify actions

Training for all

A CLASS OF THEIR OWN: THE MUSEUM AS A LEARNING RESOURCE

Northlight Productions, a broadcast and video production company specialising in educational material, was selected by Fife Museums Forum to assist in the development and the production of the video, *A Class of Their Own. The museum as a learning resource.* This professionally produced video aims to train both educators and museum staff throughout Scotland in the effective use of museum collections to support the 5–14 curriculum.

The video follows the experiences of five classes ranging from the lower primary school through to first year secondary, as they use museum objects as a source of evidence to support classroom studies across all areas of the curriculum. It highlights the opportunities for personal and social development, and for skills development, particularly with regard to the strands of Environmental Studies 5–14 and the Art & Design component of Expressive Arts 5–14. Moreover the video illustrates the benefits of forward planning by teachers, pupils and museum staff to ensure effective integration of museum studies into classroom study. Advice is given on:

- booking procedures for a visit indicating what the museum needs to know and what the teacher needs to know;
- pre-visit preparation by the teacher which might include analysis of an information pack, adapting materials produced by the museum to allow for pupil differentiation, and/or an advance visit to the museum to consider how the class visit is to be structured and to discuss requirements with museum staff;
- preparation in class – by teacher and pupils to include planning group activities and practising skills related to collecting evidence;
- managing a visit;
- consolidating a visit through follow-up activities; and
- using a loans service.

It is intended that this video will be used in museums and schools throughout Scotland as part of a staff development programme. The advice it gives on aspects of good practice in planning, preparation and follow-up work is applicable to museums and schools throughout the United Kingdom.

Video making in progress in Fife.

Part 5

"AN ASSESSMENT OF WORTH, VALUE, OR QUALITY" (Collins Dictionary 1995) Evaluation is an ongoing process at the Scottish Mining Museum

The Scottish Mining Museum is an independent museum situated at the now disused Lady Victoria Colliery at Newtongrange, Midlothian. There is no education officer, nor any other staff member with training in that field, but the Museum is fortunate in having an enthusiastic staff with a commitment to providing a service geared toward educating a variety of audiences about the significance of the Scottish coal industry. The Museum particularly focuses on school groups, the only audience to be given access to the colliery from November to February, when it is closed to the public. However, the Museum was facing a situation where the number of school groups visiting the colliery was in decline and hoped, through involvement with the Museums Education Initiative, to reverse the trend. The success of the project, *Operation Move It!*, in achieving that aim is due in no small part to their commitment to a programme of ongoing evaluation.

Generally, when people talk about evaluating a museum education service, they mean assessing a project after it is almost ended or already completed, looking back on what has been achieved and what has failed within that particular context. This type of assessment of "worth, value, or quality" is itself of limited value unless put into a broader context. If evaluation is to have true worth it must be an ongoing process, determining not only the development of a single project from start to finish, but also the continuous development of a museum education service.

It may be more constructive to redefine evaluation in terms of an information gathering exercise, carried out at three stages:

- at the planning stage of a project, as ideas begin to take shape (front-end analysis);
- during the preparation stage, as ideas take on a more concrete form (formative evaluation) and;
- on completion of a project, to sum up its impact (summative evaluation). Information gathered during the planning stage will help identify the aims and objectives, and establish a framework for the project. Information gathered and fed into the preparation stage will permit modification of the original ideas and correction of elements that are not working well, thus improving the effectiveness of the final product. Information gathered after the project is launched can be used to measure the success of the project against its original aims and objectives, and should then form the basis of further action.

These three stages should be seen as forming a continuous cycle of appraisal of museum education provision and can be undertaken by a museum service of any size, in any locality and with any type of collection, regardless of who within the service is responsible for museum education.

FRONT-END ANALYSIS

WHAT DOES IT MEAN?

Front-end analysis is really about research, gathering information during the planning of a project so that informed decisions can be taken on how to proceed. It is about making a preliminary assessment as to the needs of the target audience; how far current provision meets those needs; what has been achieved elsewhere in the proposed area for development; and what resources are available to the museum education service to support the project.

HOW IS THIS INFORMATION GATHERED?

The needs of the target audience can be identified by:

- reading relevant literature
- setting up an advisory group which consists of representatives of the target audience
- consulting representatives of the target audience on an individual basis
- circulating a questionnaire to a representative sample of the target audience.

Successes and failures in meeting the needs of the target audience can be identified by:

- observing and talking to both the target audience and staff to pinpoint both successful and unsuccessful elements of current provision at the museum
- analysing evaluation sheets
- examining summative evaluations of past experiences at the museum where these exist.

What has been achieved elsewhere can be identified by:

- reading relevant literature about the experiences of other institutions and contacting those institutions for further information where appropriate
- asking around to see if anyone has attempted something similar.

Resources available to support the project should be assessed by looking at:

- the collections, eg objects from store, handling collections, archival material, exhibitions and displays
- the buildings/site, eg what facilities and space are available
- staffing levels and expertise
- equipment available, eg audio visual, desk-top publishing
- budget.

WHAT DID IT MEAN FOR THE SCOTTISH MINING MUSEUM?

An analysis of past visitor records had shown diminishing visits from upper primary school groups, traditionally the Museum's largest school audience. The Museum considered two possible reasons for the decline. Firstly, the needs of upper primary school groups were not being sufficiently met, and secondly, the Museum's marketing strategy for schools was proving ineffective in that primary school teachers were unaware of what the Museum had to offer. The Museum determined to address each of these issues.

A questionnaire was sent out to 200 primary schools in Lothian Region in order to identify: those areas of the curriculum which primary school teachers perceived could benefit from a visit to a mining museum; the facilities of most importance to teachers in planning a visit; the methods of communication which are most effective in reaching primary school teachers; and the most effective timing for promotional material.

In the meantime, the Museum carried out research into the needs of teachers with regard to the 5–14 curriculum. An Education Working Party consisting of local teachers, members of the Scottish Consultative Council for the Curriculum, and advisory staff of Lothian Region Education Authority was formed. The Museum was

Piloting a *Source of Friction* with pupils from Newtongrange Primary School.

able to draw on the knowledge and expertise of members of this advisory group to familiarise themselves with the 5–14 documents and the implications they held for museums generally.

The results of the survey indicated that teachers saw Environmental Studies as being the area to benefit most from a visit to the Museum, particularly Social Subjects, Science and Technology. However, through discussions with the Education Working Party, it became clear that the strength of the Museum in supporting the 5–14 curriculum lay as much in its capability to provide new experiences for pupils, a context for learning, and opportunities on site to develop problem-solving and investigative skills, as in its capability to increase knowledge and understanding in subject areas. The Museum concluded that teachers would be much more likely to bring a class to the colliery if the visit involved the children in active, independent learning.

The Education Working Party also agreed with the findings of the survey in that support materials which linked the collections to the Curriculum Guidelines and provided contextual information topped the list of facilities of most importance to teachers planning a visit. Such materials would allow for preparatory work to be carried out in the classroom, ensuring integration of the visit into a cross-curricular programme of study.

Current provision and the resources available were assessed in light of these findings. A typical school visit to the colliery was analysed to identify its strengths and weaknesses. A major strength was the Museum's capability to support the Social Subjects component of Environmental Studies 5–14 with both the exhibitions and the guided tour focusing on the social history of the area. The guides themselves, all former miners at the colliery, were recognised as being a major resource for the Museum, and source of information for pupils, having a wealth of historical knowledge about the development of the coal industry. They also had a wealth of untapped technical knowledge. However, in the main, pupils were passive recipients of knowledge rather than active learners. Object handling sessions did provide the opportunity for greater interaction with the guides, but again the emphasis lay on pupils receiving information rather than finding things out for themselves. In short, while the visit was helping pupils to increase their knowledge and understanding about People in the Past, and People and Place, it was not encouraging the development of skills and independent learning. In addition, support material relating to social history for use by teachers of upper primary school pupils, predated and made no reference to the 5–14 Curriculum Guidelines.

In assessing its resources the Museum also took into consideration proposals for a major new exhibition to look at the applied Science and Technology of the Coal Industry. The research phase of the design work for the exhibition had identified approximately 10 "challenges of mining" relating to significant technological advances in the Industry's history such as transport, coal-cutting, ventilation and pumping. The results of the questionnaire had shown that primary schools recognised the potential of the Museum to support Science and Technology as components of Environmental Studies 5–14. When this exhibition was in place it would strengthen the Museum's capability to resource that area of the 5–14 curriculum, one with which many primary school teachers felt ill-equipped to deal. This could be developed alongside the Museum's other major strength, that of social history, by setting scientific and technological advances in the broad social and historical context of the impact of heavy industry on the life of the community.

Involvement in the Museums Education Initiative provided an opportunity to pilot one of the themes in advance of the new exhibition in order to provide a model both for the development of educational provision related to the exhibition and for improving existing provision. Taking into account the findings of the front-end analysis thus far, the Museum decided to modify and expand on current provision to provide a context for learning in Science and Technology which would satisfy the demand for experiential learning, and also to produce support material for teachers which would satisfy their need for preparatory resource material. The aim and objectives of the project were thus established.

Aim:
To increase the numbers of primary school groups visiting the Museum by developing an education project which satisfies the requirements of the 5–14 curriculum, and by raising awareness in teachers of what the Museum has to offer.

Objectives:
1.   To provide a context for learning in Science and Technology which brings relevance to other areas of the curriculum.
2.   To encourage the teaching and learning of investigative skills, problem solving and enquiry, working in partnership with local schools to prepare activities which allow independent teaching and learning of a range of skills at the Museum.
3.   To develop a structured support pack for teacher information which will encourage school parties to visit the Museum as an integral part of classroom study.

A lot can be learned from other people's experiences, whether those experiences be positive or negative, and at this stage other mining museums in England and Wales, and those with exhibitions related to mining in Scotland were either visited or contacted to establish whether these museums had activities on site or had produced resource materials to support Science and Technology in any shape or form. However, the Scottish Mining Museum appeared to be breaking new ground in mining museums and had to look to other museums, such as the

Fitzwilliam in Cambridge, which had developed science-based projects. They also received advice from specialist science centres, like Satrosphere in Aberdeen.

In order to select the pilot theme, a second questionnaire was distributed to a representative sample of some fifty primary school teachers who had brought school groups to the Museum the previous year, thus giving those teachers who had used the education service the opportunity to influence its development. Input from the target audience encourages a sense of joint ownership of the project, and is also an indirect means of marketing, through raising awareness of developments at the Museum. This questionnaire asked teachers to rate each of the themes in terms of their usefulness in helping pupils to achieve attainment targets as laid out in the 5–14 Guidelines for Science and Technology, and in terms of popularity of topic. There was a 50% response rate to the questionnaire. When the results were analysed, the theme of movement or transportation of coal and people from the coal-face to the surface was the preferred choice.

The next stage was to identify activities around the collections to support the theme, which would be relevant to the school curriculum. An information meeting about the project was held at the Museum, courtesy of the Teacher Placement Service, for teachers interested in being involved in its development. Two teachers from local schools showed enthusiasm for the project at the meeting and, working to a detailed brief over a period of five days each, used their classroom experience to evaluate the Museum's collections and develop the pilot theme in line with Environmental Studies 5–14 – Science and Technology. They selected five scientific principles to be investigated which related directly to the movement of coal and people through the mine and made suggestions for activities on site which would demonstrate these principles and how they influenced the development of mining technology. Friction, gravity, slopes, pulleys and gears, were all stipulated within the 5–14 Guidelines for Science, and thus regularly taught in schools. The seconded teachers also made suggestions for follow-up activities to be carried out in the classroom and links to other curricular areas. Their evaluation laid the foundation for what was to become *Operation Move It!*

FORMATIVE EVALUATION

WHAT DOES IT MEAN?
Formative evaluation involves developmental testing during the preparation stage of a project, while the work is in progress, and using the information gathered to rectify anything which is not working as planned. In this way the chance of failure is lessened.

HOW IS THIS INFORMATION GATHERED?

- Mock-ups of the exhibits/activities can be produced and tested by a sample audience to find out if they work as planned.
- A draft of any support material can be produced and made available for a sample audience to consider the content and whether the design is 'user friendly'.

WHAT DID IT MEAN FOR THE SCOTTISH MINING MUSEUM?
Having carried out the preliminary research, five large-scale working models were commissioned which would replicate the equipment and machinery used in the mines to transport people and coal which the pupils would see at first hand on their tour of the colliery. Thus the context for learning was established. Each of the models dealt with a different principle, and the idea was to set pupils an experiment which, when they carried it out, would help increase their knowledge

and understanding of that concept. However the most important aspect of the experiment was that pupils would be trying it out for themselves, encouraging skills development and independent learning.

Before the construction of the models was given the go-ahead, a mock-up of the activity based on friction was produced, and tested by from the local primary school to identify any major problems. The pupils were asked to carry out the activity without adult help and were observed while doing so. Valuable information was gathered on:

- the practicalities of pupils carrying out the activity tested, such as whether or not they could lift the boxes of coal without adult help;
- the clarity of the instructions, such as whether the pupils came to a point where they could not proceed without adult help;
- if the group worked as a team and helped each other;
- whether the language was at an appropriate level for that age group;
- what prior knowledge was necessary with regard to the equipment used and units of measurement for the pupils to be able to carry out the experiment;
- how and when the pupils used the recording sheets and whether what was recorded was the type of information expected, ie were the pupils actually understanding what problems friction caused for the miners and how they overcame it;
- whether or not the pupils were motivated to carry out the experiment to its conclusion.

After careful analysis the Scottish Mining Museum had the blueprint for the remaining four scientific principles.

Further developmental testing took place after all five large-scale interactive models had been constructed, but before *Operation Move It!* was launched. Local teachers were invited to try out the activities. They assessed whether the models were robust enough to withstand the attentions of school children; what problems they might encounter using the models; and if they were safe. A number of design faults were highlighted and subsequently rectified.

The supporting teachers' information pack was developed alongside the activities and included copies of all the background and instructional material for the experiments so that teachers would be aware of what pupils would need to know before coming to the Museum. Packs produced by a variety of museums were examined for content, curriculum alignment, design and layout. The Scottish Mining Museum combined what they considered to be the best features of each of these packs to produce a draft pack which, although focusing on Science and Technology, also gave a historical background to the development of the coal industry in Scotland in order to provide information for a cross-curricular study. The Education Working Party examined the draft, and drew attention to such things as 'differentiation', ie making sure that there was enough flexibility within the instructions for teachers to allow them to adapt the activities for children of different abilities. The pack was amended accordingly.

At last, after almost a year of combined development and evaluation, the pilot theme was ready to be launched. The results of the initial survey with regard to marketing were useful at this point. A database of 1,000 schools in areas of Scottish coal fields had been compiled. These schools were sent a full-colour information leaflet and an invitation to an 'In-sight' session at the Museum. Class teachers had been identified as being the decision makers with regard to booking visits, and those whose names were known either from previous visits or enquiries, were directly mailed.

Support packs were given to all teachers attending the awareness-raising sessions which were held in the evenings over a period of one week and also on a Saturday. Those teachers who could not attend but registered interest were also sent a pack. *Operation Move It!* was featured in the *Times Educational Supplement*, in the local press, and marketed at the Scottish CCC's Forum on Scottish Resources, held in Edinburgh.

SUMMATIVE EVALUATION

WHAT DOES IT MEAN?

Summative evaluation takes place after a project has been developed and launched. It involves gathering information which is used to assess the project against its original aims and objectives to see if it has indeed accomplished what it set out to do. It can also be used to provide information to assist in the further development of the museum education service, thus forming part of the continuous cycle of appraisal.

HOW IS THIS INFORMATION GATHERED?

Information can be gathered in a variety of ways and the most effective summative evaluation uses a combination of some or all of the following methods:

- observing the target audience during a visit and making notes of their behaviour;
- tape-recording or video-recording pupil responses during a visit;
- inviting informal verbal responses from teachers, pupils and museum staff;
- conducting in-depth interviews with teachers, pupils and museum staff;
- analysing evaluation sheets prepared for teachers and pupils;
- analysing post-visit letters from teachers and pupils;
- conducting follow-up visits to schools to look at pictures and written work of pupils produced in class;
- analysing visitor figures.

WHAT DID IT MEAN FOR THE SCOTTISH MINING MUSEUM?

In carrying out its summative evaluation the Museum used a combination of formal and informal evaluation techniques: analysing visitor figures; evaluation sheets; in-depth interviews with teachers; observation of pupils; informal comment from pupils, teachers and museum staff.

In terms of achieving its goals the project has been an unqualified success. An analysis of visitor figures has already shown a marked increase on the previous year's figures in the numbers of primary school groups visiting the colliery, thus fulfilling the aim of the project. This appears to have been achieved through a combination of more effective marketing and closer alignment to the 5–14 curriculum.

An important factor in fulfilling the first objective of the project was the decision taken by the Museum not to isolate *Operation Move It!* but to place it in among other exhibits and offer it as part of the total visit. Thus the effects of science on the development of mining technology can be seen within the broader social and historical context of mining which allows teachers to use it as part of a cross-curricular project, and to integrate it more easily into classroom study. Its inclusion as part of the tour has created problems for the guides, however, in that schools do get absorbed in the activities and are reluctant to move on. Timing of this part of the visit therefore needs to be looked at, and the role of the guides who feel that their presence is unnecessary at this point.

The second objective has been met in that the Museum did work with local schools to provide opportunities for the development of investigative and problem-solving skills stipulated in the strands of Environmental Studies 5–14. This was acknowledged by teachers in their evaluation sheets, and the capability of this active discovery learning approach to motivate pupils was evident from observation of classes using *Operation Move It!*

The third objective has been met in that all teachers who have returned evaluation sheets to date have emphasised the benefits of the support pack in helping prepare pupils for the visit, and providing contextual information which teachers have been able to use in projects which have ranged from 'Victorians' to 'Forces'.

The value of the front-end analysis and formative evaluation has been evident in the high levels of pupil and teacher satisfaction with the visit and the support materials. Attention to detail has ensured that the activites run smoothly and that pupils have no difficulties in working on them without adult help. The Museum has its model for future developments in museum education.

Operation Move It! was awarded a commendation in the Gulbenkian category for Most Imaginative Education Work, 1995.

PROJECT	CURRICULAR FOCUS	TARGET AUDIENCE	REGION	PRODUCTS	PROJECT COST	PARTNERSHIPS	CASE STUDY
Talbot Rice Gallery	Expressive Arts + Personal & Social	5–14 curr. Primary	Lothian	Artist in Residence workshops	£1,600	UBI Teacher Placement Service Local Education Authority Artist in residence Local schools	No
Marischal Museum	Environmental Studies; Social Subjects; and Technology	5–14 curr. P4–S2	Grampian	Research report	£3,000	Northern College of Education Local Education Authority Local schools Shell	Yes
Scottish Mining Museum	Environmental Studies; Science; and Technology	5–14 curr. P6–S1	Lothian	Interactive displays teachers' support pack	£5,600	Scottish CCC Local Education Authority Local schools	No
Grampian Transport Museum	Environmental Studies; Science; and Technology + links to Maths	5–14 curr. Primary	Grampian	Activities developed around teachers' support pack	£1,500	Local Education Authority Local schools BP	Yes
Earth Art: Paisley Greenock Scotland Street, Glasgow	Expressive Arts: Art & Design	5–14 curr. P7–S2 (Pri/Sec liaison)	Strathclyde	Touring exhibition Pupil/teacher resource pack Outreach ceramics workshops On-site ceramics workshops Educational Resource Service	£3,800	3 museums in Strathclyde Strathclyde Museums Education Service Strathclyde Education Development Service Street Arts Initiative Fund	Yes
The Chinese Way	Environmental Studies; Social Subjects + links to Religious & Moral Education	5–14 curr. P5–7	Strathclyde	Interactive temporary exhibition	£2,000	Strathclyde Museums Education Service Local Chinese community	Yes

PROJECT	CURRICULAR FOCUS	TARGET AUDIENCE	REGION	PRODUCTS	PROJECT COST	PARTNERSHIPS	CASE STUDY
Tweeddale Museum	Environmental Studies; Science; Technology; and Social Subjects Expressive Arts: Art & Design; Music; and Drama	5–14 curr. Primary + Special Needs	Borders	Hands-on workstations Interpretive activities Teachers' support pack Loan box	£2,850	Local Education Authority Local schools Local community groups Adult Basic Education Other museums – Biggar, Hawick, National Museums of Scotland Local artists Council for Scottish Archaeology	Yes
Western Isles	Gaelic through the context of Environmental Studies; Science with links to Social Subjects	5–14 curr. P5–S2	Western Isles	Preventive conservation activities and experiments for classroom and museum Bilingual pupil/teacher pack	£4,000	Ness Historical Society Local Education Authority Local schools	Yes
Ross & Cromarty	Training re. 5–14 curriculum		Highland	Guidelines for 5–14 curriculum for museum staff	cost of approx. £1,000 each to the six museums in the Group who participated	Ross & Cromarty Museums Network Group Ross & Cromarty Museums Service Local Education Authority UBI Teacher Placement Service Local schools Educational Resource Service	Yes
Ullapool	Higher Computer Studies	S5/6		Study re info technology/multi-media			
Gairloch	Envir. Studies	P1–3		Hands-on activities in permanent exhib.			
Dingwall	Envir. Studies	P5–7		Victorians support material			
Cromarty	Expressive Arts	P5–7		Role-play/drama activity			
Groam House	Envir. Studies	P3–S2		Pictish loan boxes			
Strathpeffer	Envir. Studies	P3–7		New displays			
Fife Museums Forum	Skills development, 5–14, with links to knowledge & understanding	5–14 curr. P1–S2	Fife	Training video	£12,000	Fife Museums Forum Local Education Authority Local schools + funding partners: Carnegie UK Trust Bank of Scotland	No
Falkirk Museums	Environmental Studies; Science; Technology; and Social Subjects	5–14 curr. P6–S2	Central	Exhibition Teachers' support pack Resource packs Loan boxes	£4,850	Local Education Authority Local schools BP	No

Bibliography

GENERAL THEORY, EDUCATIONAL ROLE OF MUSEUMS

AMERICAN ASSOCIATION OF MUSEUMS, publ.
Excellence and equity: education and the public dimension of museums. Washington, DC., American Association of Museums, 1992.

ARTS EDUCATION PARTNERSHIP WORKING GROUP
The power of the arts to transform education. An agenda for action. Recommendations from the AEPWG under the sponsorship of the John F Kennedy Center for the Performing Arts and the J Paul Getty Trust. Washington, DC, John F Kennedy Center for the Performing Arts, 1993.

BARNEA, Aviva
New Directions in Museum Education: Towards 2000. ICOM EDUCATION 14, [1994] 3–5, 3pp.

BOSDET, Mary and DURBIN, Gail, comps.
Museum education bibliography 1978-1988. Group for Education in Museums, 1989. See also annual supplements published in Journal of Education in Museums.

CLARKE, Giles
Museum Education: Deliberate and Accidental. ICOM EDUCATION 12/13, 1991, 21–23, 3pp.

COTE, Michel and VIEL, Annette, eds.
Museums: where knowledge is shared. Quebec, ICOM Canada and Canadian Museum of Civilization, 1995. Collection Museo.

GETTY CENTRE FOR EDUCATION IN THE ARTS
Discipline-based art education and cultural diversity. A national invitational seminar sponsored by the Getty Center for Education in the Arts. Austin, Texas, August 6–9 1992. Santa Monica, Ca., J Paul Getty Trust, 1993.

HARRIS, Neil
A Century of Debate. THE J PAUL GETTY TRUST BULLETIN 5:2, Spring/Summer 1990, 3–4, 2pp.

HOOPER-GREENHILL, Eilean, ed.
The educational role of the museum. London, Routledge, 1994. Leicester Readers in Museum Studies.

HOOPER-GREENHILL, Eilean
Museums and the shaping of knowledge. London, Routledge, 1991.

HOOPER-GREENHILL, Eilean, ed.
Museum, media, message. London, Routledge, 1995. Museums: New Visions / New Approaches.

HOOPER-GREENHILL, Eilean
Museums and their visitors. London, Routledge, 1994. Heritage: Care Preservation Management.

REINWARDT ACADEMY, publ.
Exhibition design as an educational tool. Leiden, Reinwardt Academy, 1983 Reinwardt Studies in Museology 1.

SADLER, Tony and MORRIS, Beryl, eds.
Museum educators think aloud on educational philosophy. Seaton, South Australia, Quoll Enterprises, 1989.

COLLECTIONS & THE CURRICULUM

ALEXANDER, Wilma, comp.
Science and technology in museums: a resource pack. Edinburgh, Scottish Museums Council, 1994.

AMBROSE, Timothy, ed.
Education in museums, museums in education. Edinburgh, HMSO, 1987.

AREA MUSEUMS SERVICE FOR SOUTH EASTERN ENGLAND
Museums and the GCSE: report from a seminar organised by AMSSEE. London, Area Museums Service for South Eastern England, 1986.

AREA MUSEUMS SERVICE FOR SOUTH EASTERN ENGLAND
Museums and the new exams. London, Area Museums Service for South Eastern England, 1988.

BOODLE, Camilla
A new decade: museums and education in the 1990s. London, National Heritage, 1992.

DORION, Christiane
Planning and evaluation of environmental education. Primary. Resource pack. Godalming, World Wide Fund for Nature, 1993.

DORION, Christiane
Planning and evaluation of environmental education. Secondary. Resource pack. Godalming, World Wide Fund for Nature, 1993.

DOWLING, Sherwood
Museum Perspectives on Technology and Education. SPECTRA 22:2, Fall 1994, 24–27, 4pp.

ELPHINSTONE, William, ed.
Pots, paintings and parasols: a teacher's guide to Fife's museums and galleries. Fife Regional Council Education Committee, 1993. Pack compiled in collaboration with Fife Museums Forum.

ENVIRONMENTAL INTERPRETATION
For the Child in Us All. ENVIRONMENTAL INTERPRETATION October 1990, 3–5, 3pp.

FIFE MUSEUMS FORUM
A class of their own: the museum as a learning resource. VHS VIDEO. Northlight Productions for Fife Museums Forum, 1995.

FRASER, Douglas
Your child learning 1: a guide for parents of children at primary school. Dundee, Scottish Consultative Committee on the Curriculum, 1993.

GOODHEW, Elizabeth
Using Natural History Collections – Focus on Education. THE BIOLOGY CURATOR 1, September 1994, 10–13, 4pp.

GREAT BRITAIN: Office of Science and Technology
Science connections. A guide to leading organisations promoting science, engineering and technology. London, HMSO, 1995.

GREAT BRITAIN: Department of Education and Science / Department for Education
HM Inspectors reports series. Series examines the use of museums by schools in England.

GREEVES, Margaret
Museums and the New Curriculum. Opportunities for the Future. SCOTTISH MUSEUM NEWS 8:2, Summer 1992, 12–13, 2pp.

HALL, Nigel, ed
Writing and designing interpretive materials for children. Manchester, Centre for Environmental Interpretation, 1984.

HILL, David A
A New Context [Effects of Education Act]. NIMROD 11, November 1993, 6–7, 2p.

HOOPER-GREENHILL, Eilean
Museum and gallery education. Leicester, Leicester University Press, 1991. Leicester Museum Studies.

HOOPER-GREENHILL, Eilean, ed.
Working in museum and gallery education: 10 career experiences. Leicester, University of Leicester Department of Museum Studies, 1992.

HOOPER-GREENHILL, Eilean, ed.
Writing a museum education policy. Leicester, Department of Museum Studies, University of Leicester, 1991.

MCBAIN, Barclay
Your child learning 2: a guide for parents of children at secondary school. Dundee, Scottish Consultative Committee on the Curriculum, 1993.

MCCLELLAND, S E
Scottish education 5–14: a parent's guide. Edinburgh, HMSO, 1993.

NEWBERY, Elizabeth and FECHER, Sarah
In the nick of time. A practical guide to teaching about conservation of objects. London, Museums & Galleries Commission, 1994.

PEARSON, Anne and ALOYSIUS, Chitra
The big foot: museums and children with learning difficulties. London, British Museum Publications, 1994.

SCHOOL CURRICULUM AND ASSESSMENT AUTHORITY, Publ.
A guide to the national curriculum for staff of museums, galleries, historic houses and sites. London, SCAA, 1995.

SCOTTISH OFFICE EDUCATION DEPARTMENT
National curriculum guidelines 5–14. Edinburgh, SOED, 1991–1993. Guidelines for each subject area.

SWORD, Frances and STEPHENSON, Philip
Science in the making. An approach to learning with objects in the Fitzwilliam Museum. Cambridge, Cambridgeshire County Council Libraries & Information Service, n.d.

WORKING GROUP FOR ENVIRONMENTAL EDUCATION
Learning for life. A national strategy for environmental education in Scotland. A report of the working group on environmental education to the Secretary of State for Scotland. Edinburgh, The Scottish Office, 1993.

PRACTICAL EXAMPLES – PARTNERSHIPS

ALBERGE, Dalya
Painting a Rosier Picture of Youth. THE TIMES 30 November 1994, 1p.

AMBROSE, Timothy, ed.
Working with museums. Edinburgh, Scottish Museums Council / HMSO, 1988.

Art Education at Summerlee. AIM BULLETIN 13:6, November 1990, 8, 1p.

BAYNES, Ken
Lessons from The Art Machine. MUSEUM DEVELOPMENT February 1992, 29–39, 11pp.

CARTER, P G
Education in independent museums. Association of Independent Museums, 1984. AIM Guideline No 6.

CONNOR, Judith L
Promoting Deeper Interest in Science. CURATOR 34:4, December 1991, 245–260, 16pp.

COOKE, Tricia
Perspectives on a Pageant. SCOTTISH MUSEUM NEWS 9:1, Spring 1993, 15, 1p.

DONNELLY, Katie
Survey of current practice in museums education in Scotland. Scottish Museums Council Museums Education Initiative. Edinburgh, Scottish Museums Council, 1993.

DR BELL'S DRAMA SCHOOL
Fu'n'skailin: primary schools drama project, Dr Bell's Drama School and Edinburgh City Museums at Lauriston Castle, 1992. VHS VIDEO. Lothian Region Education Department, 1992.

GREEVES, Margaret and MARTIN, Brian, eds.
Chalk, talk and dinosaurs? Museums and education in Scotland. Edinburgh, Moray House Publications, 1992.

GROUP FOR EDUCATION IN MUSEUMS
Museum education contacts. Milton Keynes, Museum Development Company, 1993.

HUNTER, Rachel
In Touch with the Past: Tweeddale Museum, May 1994. SCOTTISH MUSEUM NEWS 10:2, Autumn 1994, 10–12, 3pp.

IRWIN, Alan
Science at the service of the community? The Nuffield Foundation Science Shop initiative. A report on the Northern Ireland Science Shop and the Merseyside Science Shop / Interchange. London, Nuffield Foundation, 1995.

MITCHELL, Sue
Museums Education Initiative Case Studies. Edinburgh, Scottish Museums Council, 1994, 1995.

NEUMARK, Victoria
The magic exercise: twelve arts education projects. Darlington, National Association of Arts Centres, 1989.

NORTHERN COLLEGE, publ.
Exploring Scotland's historic sites. Dundee, Northern College, 1994.

OXFORD INDEPENDENT VIDEO
Strange meeting: museum, school, community – a collaboration. VHS VIDEO. Oxford, Oxford Independent Video, 1989.

PORTSMOUTH MUSEUMS
Opportunity to learn. VHS VIDEO. Portsmouth Museums Service, 1991.

RESOURCES PLUS
Directory of education - industry organisations 1995. Thatcham, Berks., Resources Plus Ltd., 1995.

SEKULES, Veronica and TICKLE, Les
Visual Art in Primary Education. MUSEUM DEVELOPMENT November 1994, 28–29, 2pp.

STONES, Judith
"An Ace Medieval Village". SCOTTISH MUSEUM NEWS 8:2, Summer 1992, 8–9, 2pp.

UPFRONT: CHOOSING THE APPROPRIATE STRATEGY

CONYBEARE, Clare, WILKINSON, Sue and ALLEN, Stephen
[Museums Association Education Survey and Report] MUSEUMS JOURNAL 93:9, September 1993, 14–15, 2p.

COPELAND, Tim
A teacher's guide to maths and the historic environment. London, English Heritage Education Service, 1991. Education on site.

DAVIDSON, Kim
Learning with objects. Aberdeen, Marischal Museum, 1994.

DERBYSHIRE MUSEUMS SERVICE
Fifty years on: a museum loans service. Published on the occasion of a seminar to mark the first delivery of museum material to Derbyshire schools in June 1937. Derby, Derbyshire Museums Service, 1987.

DURBIN, Gail, MORRIS, Susan and WILKINSON, Sue
A teacher's guide to learning from objects. London, English Heritage Education Service, 1990. Education on site.

DYER, Martin and SUMNER, Marilyn
ETHA in action: guidelines for schools and properties. Ripon, Heritage Education Trust, 1992. ETHA: Education through Heritage and the Arts.

FAIRCLOUGH, John and REDSELL, Patrick
Living history: a guide to reconstructing the past with children. London, English Heritage, 1985.

FRASER, Jemima
Do You Have Any Teachers' Packs? SCOTTISH MUSEUM NEWS Winter 1991, 3–4, 2pp.

HOOPER-GREENHILL, Eilean, ed.
Initiatives in museum education. Leicester, University of Leicester, 1989.

HOOPER-GREENHILL, Eilean, comp.
Learning and teaching with objects: a practical skills-based approach. Leicester, University of Leicester, 1988.

JAMES, Alison
The Discovery Approach at Stranraer Museum. SCOTTISH MUSEUM NEWS 8:3, Autumn 1992, 10–11, 2pp.

KEITH, Crispin
A teacher's guide to using listed buildings. London, English Heritage Education Service, 1991. Education on site.

LOTHIAN REGIONAL COUNCIL: Department of Education
A celebration of servants following the visit of George IV in 1822: a museum education/ theatre in education project at Hopetoun House, West Lothian, Spring 1985. Edinburgh, Lothian Region Education Department, 1985.

MARWICK, Sandra
Upstairs, Downstairs at Lauriston Castle in 1903. SCOTTISH MUSEUM NEWS 8:4, Winter 1992, 10–11, 2pp.

MIDDLETON, Jane
Education [Facilities for educational visits]. MUSEUMS JOURNAL 90:4, April 1990, 15, 1p.

MORRIS, Susan
A teacher's guide to using portraits. Rev ed. 1992. London, English Heritage Education Service, 1989. Education on site.

MUSEUM EDUCATION ROUNDTABLE, publ.
Patterns in practice. Selections from the Journal of Museum Education. Washington, DC, Museum Education Roundtable, 1992.

MUSEUMS JOURNAL
Special issue on museum education services. MUSEUMS JOURNAL 91:5, May 1991.

NORTHERN COLLEGE OF EDUCATION DISTANCE STUDY UNIT
Exploring the past around you. Planning and implementing a history fieldwork trail with primary pupils. Aberdeen, Northern College of Education, [1988].

O'CONNELL, Peter S
How to develop effective teacher workshops. Nashville, American Association for State and Local History, 1987. AASLH Technical Report 12.

OFFICE FOR STANDARDS IN EDUCATION
A survey of in service teacher training sessions provided by museums and galleries. A report from the Office of Her Majesty's Chief Inspector of Schools. Autumn Term 1992. London, Office for Standards in Education, 1993. Ref 292/93/NS.

STEWART, Dorothy
Building new audiences for museums. VHS VIDEO. Edinburgh, HMSO / Scottish Museums Council, 1989.

POWNALL, June and HUTSON, Nick
A teacher's guide to science and the historic environment. London, English Heritage Education Service, 1992. Education on site.

WHITE, Judith, et al.
Snakes, snails and history tails. Building discovery rooms and learning labs at the Smithsonian Institution. Washington, DC., Smithsonian Institution, 1991.

WOOD, Sydney
Understanding people in the past. A teacher's guide to Historic Scotland properties. Edinburgh, Historic Scotland, 1995.

EVALUATION

ASSOCIATION OF SCIENCE-TECHNOLOGY CENTERS, publ.
What research says about learning in science museums. Washington, DC., Association of Science-Technology Centers, 1990.

ASSOCIATION OF SCIENCE-TECHNOLOGY CENTERS, publ.
What research says about learning in science museums. Volume 2. Washington, DC., Association of Science-Technology Centers, 1993.

BORUN, Minda
Measuring the immeasurable: a pilot study of museum effectiveness. 3rd ed. Washington, D.C., Association of Science-Technology Centers, 1982.

BORUN, Minda, FLEXER, Barbara K, CASEY, Alice F and BAUM, Lynn R
Planets and pulleys: studies of class visits to science museums. Philadelphia, Franklin Institute Science Museum, 1983.

CARTER, Graham
The Importance of Role Play. ICOM EDUCATION 14, [1994] 27–30, 4pp.

CENTRE FOR LEISURE RESEARCH, EDINBURGH
An evaluation of school visits to the Gold of the Pharaohs exhibition. Edinburgh, Centre for Leisure Research, 1989.

DIAMOND, Judy
Sex Differences in Science Museums: A Review. CURATOR 37:1, 1994, 17–24, 8pp.

GOOLNIK, Janet
Hands on! Children's learning from objects in Marischal Museum. Aberdeen, Marischal Museum, 1995.

GRAHAM, Mike
Environmental Education at Towneley Hall Art Gallery and Museums, Burnley. THE BIOLOGY CURATOR 1, September 1994, 16–18, 3pp.

LEICESTER MUSEUMS, ARTS AND RECORDS SERVICES
Open eye: approaches to understanding, evaluating and making art. Leicester, Leicestershire County Council, [1991].

RUSSELL, Terry, and McMANUS, Paulette
The nature of interactive exhibits and exhibitions: towards defining objectives. Report of the conference ... Centre for Research in Primary Science and Technology ... Liverpool ... April 1987. Liverpool, University of Liverpool, n.d.

RUSSELL, Terry, VAN der WAAL, Ardrie and WHITELOCK, Marian
Evaluation of the pilot phase of the Cardiff Interactive Technology Centre "Techniquest". Liverpool University Centre for Research in Primary Science and Technology, 1988.

SCOTTISH MUSEUM NEWS
Mask-Making in a Gallery. SCOTTISH MUSEUM NEWS 9:3, Autumn 1993, 2–4, 4pp.

TUCKEY, Catherine
The primary school child at Satrosphere: what children learn from a visit to an interactive science centre. Unpublished thesis, University of Aberdeen, 1991.

Designed by HMSO Scotland. Printed for HMSO by (3808)
Dd 029 3292 C10 6/96